The Vikings in Britain and Ireland

THE UNIVERSITY OF
WINCHESTER

Martial Rose Library
Tel: 01962 827306

To be returned on or before the day marked above, subject to recall.

The British Museum

© 2014 The Trustees of the British Museum

Gareth Williams, Jayne Carroll and Stephen H. Harrison have asserted the right to be identified as the authors of this work.

Carroll's contribution to this book was undertaken during a period of teaching relief from the University of Nottingham, funded by The Leverhulme Trust in support of the interdisciplinary research programme on The Impact of Diasporas on the Making of Britain: Evidence, Memories, Inventions.

First published in 2014 by
The British Museum Press
A division of The British Museum Company Ltd
38 Russell Square, London WC1B 3QQ
britishmuseum.org/publishing

ISBN 978-0-7141-2831-3

Designed by James Alexander at JADE Design

Printed in China by Toppan Leefung Printing Ltd

The papers used by the British Museum Press are recyclable products and the manufacturing processes are expected to conform to the environmental regulations of the country of origin.

Frontispiece Part of the silver hoard from Cuerdale, Lancashire, buried AD 905–910 (see pp. 109–111). British Museum 1841,0711.1–741, 1873,1101.1; 1954,0202.1–2; 1838,0710.1436, 1442, 1168, 1203. Donated by HM Queen Victoria in 1841, in her capacity as the Duke of Lancaster.

Front cover Shetland, the closest part of the British Isles to the Viking homelands in Scandinavia, and one of the areas most densely settled by the Vikings. © The Trustees of the British Museum; photo: John Williams.

Back cover Silver penny of Sihtric Silkbeard, king of Dublin (989–1036), minted *c*.1000. The earliest coins of Sihtric, dating from *c*.997 give his name and the name of Dublin, but most of his coins, like this one, are only partially legible (see also pp. 117–119). Diam. 1.8 cm. British Museum 1986,1201.1. © The Trustees of the British Museum.

Note: Within this book, references to counties usually refer to the historical counties, rather than present-day divisions.

Contents

Who were the Vikings?

Viking is a word that, for many people, evokes an image of a fearsome male warrior, intent on ravage and plunder, fresh from a longship and poised to set fire to a monastery. There have been attempts over recent decades to replace – or at least balance – this image with one which depicts less violent Viking-Age activities: production and trade, law and administration, and aspects of everyday life in the rural and urban environments of Scandinavia and areas of Scandinavian settlement overseas. The people we call Vikings were engaged upon both sorts of activities: the monks of Britain and Ireland were right to fear the 'Danes' and 'foreigners' who engulfed their monasteries in flames, but these sea-faring Scandinavians also made significant social, cultural and economic contributions to the places in which they settled. It was, in any case, a violent age, and it was perhaps the effectiveness of Viking violence, and its imposition on places whose inhabitants were literate, that has ultimately resulted in an indelible link in the popular imagination between Vikings and bloodthirstiness (fig. 1.1).

The origin of the word *Viking* is uncertain: it has been linked to *Víken* ('The Bay'), an ancient district in southern Norway (an origin for certain 'Vikings'); more generally to the Old Norse word *vík* 'bay' (where Vikings lurked, ready to attack); and to a borrowing of Latin *vicus* 'trading place' (referring to less violent, but no less important, Viking activities). Two related words occur in texts from the Viking Age in Old Norse (the language of the Vikings): *víkingr*, referring to an individual away from home, engaged upon (probably military) endeavours as part of a group, and *víking*, referring to group activity away from home, most probably raiding, although trading may also have played a part. In Old English, the language of the Anglo-Saxons, *wicing* referred to an individual of piratical bent, sometimes, but not necessarily, one who had arrived from Scandinavia.

1.1. This nineteenth-century painting is a typical romantic image of the Vikings, focusing on the violent aspects of the Viking Age and encapsulating many associated stereotypes. Against the background of a burning monastery and murdered victims, a plundering Viking leads Christians into captivity. Lorenz Frölich, *Strandhungst*, 1883–86. Oil on canvas, 90 x 147 cm. The Museum of National History, Frederiksborg Castle, Denmark.

These words do not appear to have been in common use during the Viking Age in Britain and Ireland. In Latin texts, the raiding Scandinavians were called 'Northmen' (*Nordmanni*), 'Danes' (*Dani*), 'pirates' (*piratae*) and 'heathens' (*pagani*). Old English texts refer to 'Danes' (*Dene*), 'Northmen' (*Norðmenn*), and 'heathens' (*hæðene*). 'Danes' and 'Northmen' have broadly the same meaning – raiders from Scandinavia – rather than referring to distinct ethnic groups. In Welsh and Old Irish sources, the Vikings are usually 'foreigners' (Welsh *gint*; Irish *gaill*), and 'light/white' and 'dark/black' groups are distinguished. The exact significance of this is disputed: it may be an ethnic distinction (perhaps Norwegians versus Danes), or the distinction may lie in some other aspect of identity, clear to Irish and Welsh chroniclers but obscure to a twenty-first-century audience. Some Irish medieval sources also use the Old Irish word *genti* (literally 'gentiles'), implying foreigners with 'pagan' beliefs.

The absence of a clear alternative has contributed to the use of the word Viking in a broader sense in modern English. Denmark, Norway and Sweden were only emerging as unified kingdoms in the Viking Age, and labelling groups and individuals as Danes or Norwegians implies both a precision and an identity which are quite anachronistic even for the Scandinavian homelands, let alone the population of the wider Viking world, which had close contacts with many different ethnic and cultural groups. This interaction often resulted in populations of mixed descent. In the absence of any other word which captures both the inhabitants of Scandinavia and the wider scattering of people linked with Scandinavia from the late eighth to the eleventh centuries, the term Viking has acquired this more general meaning. This is the sense in which the term is usually applied throughout this book, even if few of the people discussed here would have described themselves as Vikings.

The Viking Age

It is difficult to place precise dates on the beginning and end of the Viking Age, but the round dates of AD 800–1050 or 1100 work reasonably well. Archaeological evidence indicates that there was contact between

1.2. Carved stone, probably a grave marker, from Lindisfarne, Northumbria, England. The carving shows warriors with swords and axes and is often interpreted as an image of the Viking raid of AD 793. It is broadly from the right period, although the absence of any inscription means that this association cannot be proven. H. 28 cm; W. 42 cm. Lindisfarne Priory Museum.

The Vikings in Britain and Ireland

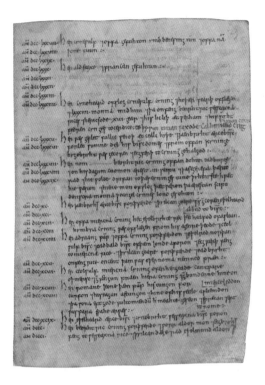

1.3. The earliest surviving copy of the *Anglo-Saxon Chronicle* is preserved in Cambridge, Corpus Christi College manuscript 173. This folio (11r) includes the entry dated 787, which records the arrival of three ships, 'the first ships of Danish men to have sought the land of the English', at some point between 786 and 802.

Britain and Scandinavia well before 800, and the early raids were probably prompted, at least in part, by an awareness of both the wealth and the vulnerability of churches and monasteries around the coasts of Britain and Ireland. Many of these religious houses were placed in relatively remote places to avoid too much contact with the secular world, making them an easy target for raiders from the sea.

One such raid on the monastery of Lindisfarne off the coast of Northumbria, England in 793 is often taken as the starting point of the Viking Age, primarily because the attack was described in dramatic terms by contemporaries (fig. 1.2). In fact, a potentially earlier attack is recorded on the coast of Dorset, England in the *Anglo-Saxon Chronicle*, although this is not precisely dated (fig. 1.3). In any case, it generated less outrage than the attack on Lindisfarne, probably because it did not involve a church. Earlier attacks in other places may have passed

Who were the Vikings?

9

unrecorded, especially given the proximity of western Norway to the Northern Isles of Scotland, and the shortage of contemporary records for Scotland in the Viking Age (see p. 40). Raids on churches by Christians were rare (although not unknown, especially in Ireland) but the attack on Lindisfarne attracted attention because of the lack of respect for the Church rather than because the attackers came from Scandinavia. Such attacks were to become more frequent, but continued to be recorded as shocking atrocities, especially by churchmen with direct connections with the churches and monasteries concerned.

The reason for the beginning of the Viking expansion has been debated by historians and archaeologists, and there is no consensus. It has been explained in terms of a pagan reaction to aggressive Christian missionary activity on the Continent, but this view has not been widely accepted in recent years. Another interpretation links the raids with developments in the design of Viking ships, although this view has largely been rejected in the face of increasing evidence of contact long before the raids began. Over-population in Scandinavia also seems unlikely as a driver for the early raids, since (with the possible exception of northern

1.4. Gilt silver cup from Halton Moor, Lancashire, England. The cup is of Frankish (Continental) workmanship, dating from the mid ninth century and was probably looted from a church or monastery, remaining in Viking hands until it was buried as part of a hoard in the 1020s. H. 9.5 cm. British Museum AF.541. Bequeathed by Sir Augustus Wollaston Franks.

Scotland) the early raids seem to have focused on hit and run attacks, rather than settlement. It seems more likely that the early raids were aimed primarily at the acquisition of wealth, in order to maintain and increase the status of the raiders within their own society. The practice of dividing inheritances between several relatives in Scandinavia meant that a family's wealth would be spread more thinly with each generation unless new sources of wealth could be found.

If the beginning of the Viking Age is hard to define, the same is true of the end. From an English perspective, the failed invasion of Harald Hardruler (*harðráði*) of Norway in 1066 is often quoted as the end date, but this should perhaps be seen as a war between two kingdoms rather than a Viking raid, and there were later raids by both Danish and Norwegian kings. Elsewhere in Britain and Ireland this date has even less significance. Magnus Barelegs (born *c.*1073), king of Norway from 1095, died while raiding in Ulster, Ireland in AD 1103, and raids on Wales continued into the twelfth century. Dublin remained at least partly Scandinavian (if increasingly dominated by Irish kings) until the Anglo-Normans took the city in 1170, while the Isle of Man and the Hebrides remained under Norwegian rule until 1266, and the Orkney and Shetland islands until 1468 and 1469 respectively. However, so many aspects of society had changed by the mid eleventh century, both in the Scandinavian homelands and in settlements abroad, that it can be argued that these areas had lost their 'Viking' character by then. Approximate end dates of 1050 or 1100 are therefore generally accepted for the Viking Age.

1.5. Silver pendant from Little Snoring in Norfolk, England. Probably made in Scandinavia in the tenth century, it is in the 'Borre style' – a type of animal ornamentation – and has close parallels with finds from Norway and Sweden. H. 4.2 cm. British Museum 1999,1001.1.

The Vikings came from what are now the countries of Denmark, Norway and Sweden, although these kingdoms only took shape in the course of the Viking Age, and their modern boundaries were not finally established until centuries later. Kings of the 'Danes' are recorded before the Viking Age, but this does not mean that they controlled the whole of modern Denmark, which may initially have been divided into

1.6. Runestone at Jelling, Denmark. This stone, raised by King Harald Bluetooth, ostensibly in memory of his father Gorm and his mother Thyre, bears an inscription claiming that Harald 'won for himself all of Denmark and Norway, and made the Danes Christian.'

smaller kingdoms. The landscape lends itself to this as, apart from the Jutland peninsula in the west, Denmark is made up of separate islands of various sizes. There is evidence of the kings of the Danes having strong power in Jutland by the eighth century, and by the mid tenth century King Harald Bluetooth (reigned *c*.958–*c*.986) was able to proclaim on a runestone at Jelling that he had 'won all of Denmark for himself', as well as at least part of Norway (fig. 1.6). By the end of the tenth century, Danish kings also ruled parts of what is now southern Sweden, and this may already have been the case under Harald.

Norway was also fragmented both politically and geographically. Although most of what later became this kingdom formed a continuous strip extending along the coast from the Oslo Fjord in the south to territories beyond the Arctic Circle, it was naturally divided by mountains and fjords, with a large number of small islands along the coast. These natural units formed a series of small kingdoms that were only gradually united. South-eastern Norway intermittently came under Danish control, and Danish power occasionally extended further, as under Harald Bluetooth, and Cnut the Great (see pp. 31 and 117). Later tradition suggested that Norway was united around 870 by Harald Finehair, but the dates of Harald's reign are problematic and while there is some evidence to support consolidation of power in western Norway at that time, Norway was not fully unified until the eleventh century.

Sweden was divided to a lesser extent by mountains and forest. There were two main peoples, the Svear in Uppland in the east, and the Götar in the south and west. Again, there was unification of sorts in the late tenth and eleventh centuries, but this broke down fairly quickly, and lasting integration only came after the Viking Age.

In addition to the Nordic peoples who lived in all three kingdoms, and who spoke languages derived from a common ancestor (Danish, Norwegian and Swedish remain very similar even today), there were also a number of other peoples living in northern Norway and Sweden. Contemporary accounts refer to *Finnas*, *Terfinnas*, *Cwenas* and *Beormas*. Relatively little is known about these groups, since they have left no written records and there is little archaeological evidence, but they appear to have been nomadic or semi-nomadic peoples related to the Finns of Finland, and also to the modern Sámi people of northern Norway and Sweden.

1.7. Single-edged iron sword blade from Digeråkeren, Norway. The *langsax*, or single-edged sword, is characteristic of Norway in the early Viking Age, although double-edged swords are generally more common across the Viking world. Seventh to ninth centuries. L. 97 cm. British Museum 1891,1021.27.

Finds of looted metalwork (p. 22) suggest that the earliest raids on the British Isles came from south-western Norway, and the bulk of the Viking raids and settlement in the west seems to have come from Denmark and Norway, while the Swedes were more involved in expansion to the east. However, there was no straightforward division. Several Swedish runestones refer to individuals who had raided in England (see pp. 60–63), and many Viking raiding bands must have been composed of mixtures of different peoples from around the Viking homelands.

Viking Ships

The physical fragmentation of the Scandinavian homelands meant that they were both divided and connected by the sea. There were relatively few areas in which it was possible to travel more quickly and easily over any substantial distance by land rather than by river, fjord or sea. This meant that ships and seamanship were central to Scandinavian society. This was already true before the Viking Age, but developments in shipbuilding contributed to a Viking expansion which eventually spanned four continents.

Ships were no less important for the Vikings in Britain and Ireland. Navigable rivers allowed them to penetrate far inland on their raids, and it is no coincidence that many of the areas that they settled were on islands or around the coast and along major rivers. The North Sea connected Britain with Scandinavia, while the Irish Sea connected Viking settlements in the north-west of England, Ireland, Scotland, Wales and the Isle of Man.

The Vikings brought their shipbuilding traditions with them. Their ships were clinker-built, with hulls made of overlapping planks reinforced by internal ribs, unlike some other ship-types where the main strength was in a heavy frame, to which the hull planks were then attached. The result was ships that were relatively light and flexible for their size, allowing them to travel along rivers as well as by sea, and to pull up on shallow beaches rather than requiring deep harbours.

A number of Viking ships are known from burials, in which the ship provided a tomb for the deceased and perhaps symbolic transportation to the afterlife. Smaller 'boat' graves have been found in Scotland and on the Isle of Man. Other ships and boats were wrecked, and others again were deliberately sunk to block sailing channels and control access to important settlements. The surviving examples show considerable variation in size and type, and this almost certainly reflects the continuing development of ship design throughout the Viking Age. One of the largest known Viking ships, *Skuldelev 2*, was built in the Dublin area, even though it was discovered in Denmark (fig. 1.8).

1.8. The *Sea Stallion from Glendalough* is a reconstruction of the Viking warship *Skuldelev 2*, which was built in the Dublin area and found in Roskilde Fjord, Denmark. L. c. 30 m.

Early ships, mostly known from burials in Norway, seem to have combined moderately large crews (allowing them to be rowed or sailed) with a reasonable carrying capacity for cargo, loot, or stores. Later ships fall into two major types – long, narrow warships carrying large crews but with little space for anything else, and deeper, broader cargo ships with more carrying capacity, but with fewer oars and smaller crews. The variation in size also meant that some ships and boats were only suitable for use in relatively sheltered waters, while others were designed for the open sea and were even capable of crossing the Atlantic.

The Viking ships placed Scandinavia at the heart of an international network of contacts, which extended further than that of any previous medieval society. The North Sea provided an obvious link to the west, and trade and exchange networks had already been established before the beginning of the Viking Age. This brought the Vikings into contact with the Anglo-Saxons, Picts, Frisians and Franks, who occupied territories broadly corresponding to parts of modern England, Scotland, the Netherlands, Belgium, Germany and France. From the North Sea it was a natural extension to sail round either the north of Scotland or south of England, enabling contact with western Britain and Ireland.

However, journeys to the west also went much further afield. Some Vikings continued south, along the Atlantic seaboard of what is now France, Spain and Portugal until they reached the Straits of Gibraltar. This brought them into contact with the Islamic inhabitants of southern Spain and North Africa, and provided access to the Mediterranean. In the North Atlantic, they were able to expand into the largely unoccupied islands of the Faroes and Iceland, and to establish settlements in southern Greenland. Both written and archaeological evidence show that they reached North America and interacted with the native inhabitants, but this does not appear to have led to lasting settlement.

As the North Sea provided the opportunity for contact with and expansion to the west, so did the Baltic to the east, and archaeological evidence makes it clear that, again, Scandinavians had established contacts with the southern and eastern coasts before the Viking Age. The shallow draught (depth) of their ships enabled them to travel along great rivers such as the Dvina, the Dniepr and the Volkhov, traversing

1.10. *Overleaf* The Vale of York Hoard, buried in 927–8, symbolizes the cultural contacts of the Viking world. Almost the entire hoard was packed inside a gilt-silver Frankish church vessel. It included Anglo-Saxon, Viking, Frankish and Islamic coins, together with metalwork from Britain, Ireland, Scandinavia and Russia. British Museum 2009,8023.1–76 and 2009,4133.77–693. Purchased with assistance from the Art Fund and the National Heritage Memorial Fund.

modern Latvia, Belorussia, the Ukraine, and Russia. The name 'Rus' probably applied originally to a people in or from eastern Sweden, but as they pushed east they mingled with Slavs and a variety of other ethnic groups to provide the origins of the 'Russian' people.

The upper reaches of the rivers connecting with the Baltic were separated by only a short distance from other rivers leading south to the Black Sea and the Caspian Sea. These rivers provided valuable trade routes through the territories controlled by a number of nomadic or semi-nomadic peoples originally from Central Asia, including the Khazars, the Pechenegs and the Volga Bulghars. Crucially, these routes also provided contacts with two great empires further south: the Byzantine Empire, with its capital at Constantinople (modern Istanbul), and the eastern part of the Islamic Caliphate which extended from the Middle East as far as modern Afghanistan, as well as all the way around the southern Mediterranean to Spain. The Viking settlements in Britain and Ireland thus sat towards the western edge of a Viking world which extended far beyond northern Europe and the North Atlantic.

1.9. Gilt copper-alloy brooch from Ballycottin, Ireland. The brooch is Frankish, dating from the eighth to ninth centuries. In the centre is a re-used stone with an Arabic inscription, showing links to the Islamic world. L. 4.4 cm. British Museum 1875,1211.1. Donated by Philip T. Gardner.

Raiding and warfare

The earliest firmly dated 'Viking' raid in western Europe occurred in Northumbria, England in 793, when the island monastery of Lindisfarne was sacked. This caused the Anglo-Saxon monk Alcuin, then resident in the court of Charlemagne, or Charles the Great (died 814), king of the Franks from 768, and emperor from 800, to write to Ethelred, king of Northumbria (reigned AD 774–779 and 790–796):

> *...never before has such terror appeared in Britain as we have now suffered ... Behold, the church of St Cuthbert spattered with the blood of the priests of God, despoiled of all its ornaments; a place more venerable than all in Britain is given as a prey to pagan peoples.*

Two years later, in 795, Viking raiders attacked the Irish monastery of *Rechru*, probably Rathlin Island, off the north-east coast of Antrim. While records for Scotland at this time are almost non-existent, there can be little doubt that raiding had already occurred there, and Iona, a particularly important monastery in the Western Isles with strong Irish connections, was raided four times between 795 and 826, by which time at least some of its community had fled to Kells, County Meath.

These early raids, however, were very irregular, and until the 830s there were years in which no raids whatsoever were noted in the Irish annals, a group of closely-related yearly records kept at some monasteries. The *Anglo-Saxon Chronicle* is also silent on the subject for much of the first half of the ninth century, although this may reflect that source's strong bias towards Wessex, one of the areas in England furthest from Scandinavia. Such raids as were recorded seem to have been carried out by single ships or small fleets of perhaps three vessels, suggesting raiding parties of less than a hundred men. Monasteries seem to have been prime targets, although their literate inhabitants were also those most able to record their misfortunes. As major centres of wealth and population, these sites, particularly those in coastal locations or on navigable rivers, were clearly tempting for the first Viking raiders.

2.1. Clonmacnoise, County Offaly. One of the most important monastic sites in early medieval Ireland, its location on a major river (the Shannon) made it an easy target. The first recorded Viking raid on the site took place in AD 842. The Cross of the Scriptures (shown here) was erected some sixty years later, and reflects the monastery's continuing prosperity.

The Vikings in Britain and Ireland

2.2. Gilt copper-alloy mount, found in the Phoenix Park, Dublin. Dating to the eighth century and made to be attached to a rectangular object, such as a shrine or book cover, this artefact, like many in Scandinavia, was recovered from the furnished grave of a woman (see also fig. 3.6). L. (of longest straight side) 4.9 cm. British Museum 1854,0307.3.

Viking loot

The most obvious form of ecclesiastical loot are the pieces of Irish and Anglo-Saxon metalwork which regularly turn up in Viking graves in Norway and indeed in Britain and Ireland. The bullion value of most of these objects was relatively low, which may explain why some of them have survived more or less intact (fig. 2.2), and others have been modified to form brooches. These 'insular' brooches (i.e. from Britain and Ireland) seem to have been particularly fashionable in the ninth century, and it is interesting to note that the majority of insular artefacts in Norway come from women's graves. It has even been suggested that many raiders were seeking the 'bride price' necessary to marry.

Metalwork was not the only target for raiders. When, in 866, a series of Viking bases around the north coast of Ireland were attacked and plundered by Irish forces, large numbers of cattle and sheep were recovered. Cows were both a source and symbol of wealth in early medieval Ireland, but it is by no means clear how large numbers of these animals could have been transported back to Scandinavia by raiders. Ransom or other forms of extortion were also practised. A marginal inscription in the *Codex Aureus*, a richly decorated gospel-book, tells us it was ransomed 'from the heathen army with pure gold' by a pious Anglo-Saxon and his wife. Important captives were also often ransomed, but less fortunate individuals may well have ended their days as Viking slaves. The Vikings sometimes targeted monastic sites on feast days, and this may reflect a desire to capture large numbers of people, presumably with a view to enslaving them. However, while slavery was a fact of life in the Viking Age, its scale remains the subject of debate (see p. 123).

Those whom the Vikings attacked were quick to accuse them of a range of atrocities, primarily against the Church. To Christian commentators, the desecration of church sites was every bit as much a crime as theft or murder, but it should be noted that the number of churches known to have been permanently destroyed by the Vikings was relatively small. It was undoubtedly the fear of continuing attacks that led some small groups of monks to relocate their monasteries to more secure locations, such as Durham or Kells. Archaeological evidence for Viking raids is, however, thin on the ground, and can often be interpreted in different ways. Layers of charcoal at a number of church sites, for example, may be the result of accidental fires rather than Viking activity. Even skeletal evidence can be problematic, as at Donnybrook, Dublin, where a low mound long interpreted as the site of a Viking massacre is now believed to be an Irish cemetery containing a single Viking grave.

The advent of radiocarbon dating has allowed a number of unaccompanied and often informal burials to be linked to the Viking Age, where they are often assumed to be the victims of raids. Certainly, the five individuals buried unceremoniously in a ditch at Llanbedrgoch, Anglesey, Wales, met an unfortunate violent end, but it is perhaps typical of the period that opinion is divided as to whether these skeletons are

2.3. The Llanbedrgoch burials in Anglesey, Wales. During excavations in 1998 and 1999, a total of five skeletons were found in the upper fill of the ditch surrounding this settlement site. Two of the adults – both men – may have had their hands tied. Their deaths are assumed to be related to a raid by, or on, a Viking group.

the remains of Vikings or their victims (fig. 2.3). After all, any Viking who fell into the hands of a local ruler following an unsuccessful raid or battle could expect little mercy – unless, of course, there was a political advantage in ransoming or releasing them.

Viking warriors

Much has been written about the Vikings' military prowess, but most of it was recorded long after the Viking Age. The thirteenth-century Icelandic sagas portray a society in which military ability was a valued male attribute (see p. 33), and fighting was sometimes necessary to maintain or increase status, to protect family property and rights, or to fulfil social obligations. By no means all 'Vikings' were warriors by profession, however. There must have been many who never raided, while for many others, raiding was an activity undertaken on one or two occasions when young.

For some, though, warfare became a way of life. Unless the population of the 'Great Army' (see p. 26) was exceptionally unstable, those who fought their way across England between 865 and 880 would have spent as many as fifteen years engaged in military activity, and their abilities must have increased as a result. Other Viking leaders attracted substantial forces that travelled with them, and even relatively minor Viking kings, earls and chieftains would have had semi-permanent groups of warriors in attendance. Such men must have formed the core of most armies.

Viking society was far from unique in early medieval Europe; in fact many of the groups with which the Vikings came into contact were governed by elites with similar values and a comparable attitude to military ability. The Vikings had no great technological advantages, but there were clearly occasions when they exploited local circumstances, making and breaking alliances to their own ends. For a brief period, too, the Vikings' ability to carry out fast raids from the sea, departing before a local king could muster forces to oppose them, was a major advantage. Even in this early period, however, raids were not always successful, and as the scale of attacks grew, so too did the associated risks. Across Britain and Ireland, records make it clear that raids and battles could sometimes go terribly wrong for the Vikings instead of for their intended victims.

From the mid ninth century onwards, raiding parties began to increase in size, and Anglo-Saxon, Irish and Frankish (Continental) sources refer to fleets of tens or even hundreds of ships. This meant that the number of men involved could have been hundreds or even thousands. Rather than simple hit and run raids on individual towns or monasteries, these raids often targeted larger areas, destabilizing entire kingdoms. In 865, a force described as *se micel here* (normally translated as 'the Great Army') arrived in East Anglia, and campaigned for more than a decade. There seem to have been a number of leaders in temporary alliance, as several kings and earls are mentioned at different points. By 874 the Great Army had conquered Northumbria, East Anglia and parts of Mercia, three out of the four main kingdoms in Anglo-Saxon England. Part of the Great Army continued their attempts to conquer the remaining Anglo-Saxon kingdom of Wessex, but they were defeated in 878 by its king, Alfred (reigned 871–99), subsequently known as 'the

2.4. Chess pieces from the Isle of Lewis. Made in Norway in the twelfth century, after the Viking Age, the weapons and equipment of these armed figures are not particularly Scandinavian but conform to north European norms at the time. However, the fact that they are biting their shields may relate to later legends of the 'berserk' battle frenzy of the Vikings. H. 9.2 cm. British Museum 1831,1101.123–125.

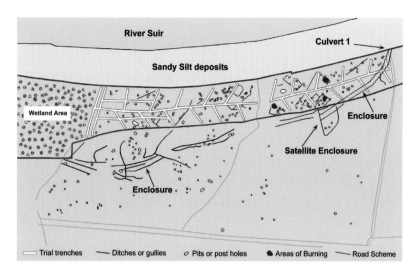

2.5. Plan of Woodstown, County Waterford, Ireland. This roughly D-shaped enclosure is situated at the point where a small tributary (the 'wetland area') enters the larger River Suir. As such, it is typical of many *longphuirt* sites. A Viking grave was found just outside the enclosure, at the point marked Culvert 1.

Great' for his success against the Vikings. Other assaults around the Irish Sea were more successful, and a key figure, Ivarr 'the Boneless', was later remembered as the founder of the royal dynasty of Viking Dublin. Although the historical evidence is less reliable, it was probably around the same time that the Vikings took control of the Northern and Western Isles of Scotland.

Longphuirt and other defended sites

With the more prolonged campaigns in the mid ninth century came the development of semi-permanent defended bases. The origin of these defended sites is unclear – fortifications are exceptionally rare in Viking-Age Scandinavia, and their inspiration may actually have come from contacts with Western Europe. Some of these sites were only occupied for short periods. One of the best known examples, at Repton, Derbyshire, England, was occupied for the winter of 873–4, forming a temporary base for the Great Army. Others, notably Dublin, were occupied for decades, although it must be assumed that much of their population was transient.

Irish commentators called these sites *longphuirt* (sg. *longphort*), a word which meant 'ship-landing', but which seems to have had a military connotation almost from the beginning. While there are exceptions, these sites seem, typically, to have consisted of earthen ramparts (banks) created on the shore of a navigable river, often where a smaller tributary provided additional defence on one side. Woodstown, County Waterford, Ireland, is one of the few examples where limited excavations have taken place (fig. 2.5). The settlement was clearly prosperous, if relatively short-lived, with evidence for commercial exchange and extensive manufacturing, including metalworking and ship repair. Oddly, the

2.6. Finds from a Viking camp in North Yorkshire, England. The finds recorded from the site include the remains of two swords (hilt or handle fragments from one appear on the right of the image) and an axe, as well as evidence of both production and trade, including coins, weights, and fragments of silver and other metals. British Museum.

The Vikings in Britain and Ireland

surviving Irish records make no explicit reference to this site. This is also the case with a comparable site in North Yorkshire, England, which apparently had a similar character (fig. 2.6). However, the archaeological evidence makes it clear that some of these fortifications had considerable economic as well as military importance, even if few were to develop into towns in the later Viking Age.

Towns did develop, in part as defensive structures, in areas of Viking settlement in England, and around the coast of Ireland (see pp. 88–9), although not in Viking Scotland. The towns served as a focus for control of the surrounding area, and the fortunes of Viking settlement in England and Ireland in the tenth century largely depended on the ability to defend these emerging towns. The Irish annals record the expulsion of the 'foreigners' from Dublin in 902, although archaeology does not currently suggest a break in settlement, and it was members of the same dynasty who re-established control there from 917 onwards. In England, the *Anglo-Saxon Chronicle* records the submission one by one of the 'armies' attached to individual towns between the River Thames and the Humber estuary in the face of West-Saxon expansion from the reign of Alfred onwards. As the only Anglo-Saxon kingdom to survive the depredations of the 'Great Army', Wessex was ideally positioned to expand its authority.

This West-Saxon conquest of the Viking territories led to the unification of England under Athelstan (924/5–939). Athelstan's rule was challenged, and at the Battle of Brunanburh in 937 he faced an alliance of Dublin Vikings, Strathclyde Britons and Scots, a reminder that the native Christian rulers of the British Isles were often happy to ally with Vikings against each other. The location of Brunanburh remains hotly debated (most recent commentaries place the battle either in the Wirral in north-west England, or near the Humber on the east coast of northern England), but the battle was a major victory for Athelstan. However, following Athelstan's death in 939 the north of England again became a battleground between Athelstan's successors and Viking leaders from Dublin and elsewhere. This phase of conflict ended with the re-establishment of English rule following the expulsion and killing of the Viking ruler Eric Bloodaxe of Northumbria in 954.

2.7. Statue of Ealdorman Byrhtnoth at Maldon, Essex, by John Doubleday, 2006. H. of statue (excl. plinth) 2.7 m. Although Byrhtnoth was defeated by a Viking army close to this site in 991, the battle was commemorated in verse soon afterwards, perhaps in part because it could be contrasted with the equally unsuccessful policy of paying the Vikings to leave England peacefully.

Eric's death has often been taken as the end of a 'First Viking Age' in England, but this label does not really make sense elsewhere. Raiding in Ireland continued, and the Viking kingdom of Dublin remained an independent political force well into the eleventh century. The same period also saw the expansion of authority around the Irish Sea by Viking kings based in the Isle of Man, and in Scotland by the earls of Orkney. The relative peace in England probably reflects the strength of English royal power, rather than a lack of Viking activity. A poem about the Anglo-Saxon king Edgar (959–75) claims that no fleet dared to attack England during his reign, implying that they might have done had it not been for Edgar's power.

Raiding in England on a large scale returned in 991, with an attack on the south-east. Following initial raids around the Kentish coast, the Viking fleet landed at Maldon in Essex, where they were met by Byrhtnoth, ealdorman of Essex (fig. 2.7). The battle is commemorated in a poem written a few years later, which provides one of the most detailed near-contemporary accounts of a battle in the Viking Age. Byrhtnoth was killed, and his army defeated, and the Anglo-Saxon King Ethelred II (reigned 978–1016) was obliged to pay tribute to the Vikings in return for peace. This was the first of many such payments, known as *gelds*, during Ethelred's reign, but these did nothing to prevent further raids, and eventually raiding turned to conquest. In 1013 Svein Forkbeard, king of Denmark, conquered England and, although he died shortly afterwards (1014) and Ethelred briefly returned, Svein's son Cnut (died 1035) took command of his father's army and established more lasting authority in 1016. He subsequently became king of Denmark and conquered parts of Norway, and later sources suggest that he also had some authority over the Scandinavian settlements in Scotland and around the Irish Sea.

Warfare and poetry

Cranes of battle flew
over piles of carrion;
the mouths of the wound-gull
did not want for blood.
The ravenous one tore the wound,
and wave of the spear-point
roared on the raven's
head-prow.

[*cranes of battle* = ravens, *wound-gull* = raven,
the ravenous one = a wolf, *wave of the spear-point*
= blood, *head-prow (of the raven)* = beak]

The lines given above are from the poem *Hǫfuðlausn* ('Head Ransom'), which according to saga tradition was composed and recited in the tenth century by Egill Skallagrimsson (fig. 2.8) for Eric Bloodaxe in York. They give a good idea of some of the ways in which battle-prowess is conveyed in the tradition of Old Norse poetry known as 'skaldic' (from the Old Norse word *skald*, 'poet'). Skaldic verse is intricately structured: alliteration and internal rhymes and half-rhymes are combined within syllable-restricted lines. These 'fix' the text, making it easier to remember and difficult to alter. Much of its vocabulary is specifically poetic and obscure to a modern-day reader, and it makes use of complex metaphors, known as *kennings*.

Hǫfuðlausn is unusual in using end-rhyme (in the Old Norse version), but its descriptions of battle-scenes are highly traditional in their use of kennings and *heiti*, specifically poetic terms. In this stanza we find two of the three conventional Germanic beasts of battle, the raven and the wolf, though not the eagle. Here, ravens are referred to in two kennings, 'cranes of battle' and 'wound-gull', and a wolf with the *heiti*-term *freki*, translated above as 'the ravenous one'. Freki is also the name of one of the two wolves of Norse mythology which are said to accompany the god Odin: the poem *Grímnismál* tells us, 'Geri and Freki the battle-accustomed father of hosts feeds, but on wine alone splendidly weaponed Odin ever lives'. Though Egill's stanza lacks specific detail, it is effective in giving an overall impression of widespread battle-carnage. It has more subtle effects too: the kennings of the stanza's second half turn blood to sea, in an extended sea-faring metaphor which continues a series of liquid- and sea-images that suffuse the whole poem.

2.8. The warrior-poet Egill Skallagrimsson, as illustrated in the seventeenth-century manuscript of *Egils saga*. The saga itself was compiled in the thirteenth century, and incorporates poems from the tenth century. The style of Egill's sword and costume are out of keeping with the Viking period, reflecting the late date of the manuscript. The Árni Magnússon Institute, Reykjavík, Iceland. AM 426 fol.,f.2v.

Weaponry

The Viking practice of placing weapons in the graves of some high-status men means that we know far more about their weapons than those of their Christian opponents. For some reason, armour was rarely deposited in these graves. Shields, on the other hand, were frequent grave-goods, although only the metal boss from the centre of the wooden shield-board regularly survives (fig. 2.9). Offensive weapons deposited in graves corresponded to what would later be called the *folkvápn* – swords, spears and axes – with occasional arrowheads.

2.9. Viking shield boss from Boldstad, Norway. Ninth to tenth century. Fixed to the centre of a round wooden shield-board, the hemispherical iron boss helped to protect the hand where it gripped the shield. Diam. 13.7 cm. British Museum 1891,1021.44.

Only the very richest could afford swords. Some of the earliest examples were single-edged (fig. 1.7), but double-edged swords were always present, and soon came to dominate completely (fig. 2.10). Both were slashing weapons with blades which were difficult to manufacture. The finest examples were pattern-welded in a technique which combined excellent qualities with a decorative appearance. The best blades were produced in the Rhineland (now in western Germany), but nonetheless made their way into Scandinavian hands. These high-quality blades are often associated with spectacular hilts (handles), clearly designed to impress.

Spearheads were sometimes pattern-welded or decorated in some other way, but the majority were purely functional. They were far more common than swords and seem to have been used both for hand-to-hand combat and (more rarely) for throwing. Interestingly, some Viking groups in Britain and Ireland adopted local Irish or Anglo-Saxon spears

2.10. Viking-Age sword. Swords were the most prestigious of Viking-Age weapons, and elaborate hilts (handles) such as the one shown here are not uncommon finds. The blade is double-edged. Tenth century, found in London. L. 88.5 cm. British Museum 1887,0209.1. Bequeathed by Henry Dunbar Baines through Rev. J.C. Jackson.

or spear forms, either because they conferred some advantage in local warfare or because no other types were available. Axeheads, on the other hand, are rare in insular contexts in the early Viking Age, although they became more common later on. They do not seem to have been used by local groups before the arrival of the Vikings, but were adopted by both Irish and Anglo-Saxon groups before the end of the period.

2.11. Iron spear- and axeheads, both from London. Tenth to eleventh century. Large spearheads such as this were used in hand-to-hand combat rather than as throwing weapons. Axeheads were relatively rare in early Viking-Age Britain and Ireland, but became increasingly common as time progressed. L. 37.9 cm and 21.5 cm. British Museum 1856,0701.1452 and 1909,0626.8.

The Battle of Clontarf

Clontarf is, without doubt, the best known Irish battle of the Middle Ages. Fought on open ground a short distance north-east of Dublin on Good Friday (23 April) 1014, it has been the subject of antiquarian and historical attention for almost a millennium (fig. 2.12, *overleaf*). Approximately a century after the battle, in the court of Muirchertach Ua Briain, king of Ireland, the *Cogadh Gáedhel re Gallaibh* – 'The War of the Irish with the Foreigners' – was composed by a scribe who saw Clontarf as the culmination of the career of Brian Bórama (or Boru), Muirchertach's great-grandfather. The battle is portrayed as an epic struggle between the Christian king Brian and a host of foreign pagans, aided by a group of disloyal vassals. The resulting tale of an Irish struggle against foreign opponents had an enormous appeal for nineteenth-century nationalists, who reinterpreted the story according to their own values. Brian died a martyr's death, while the foreigners were utterly defeated and driven into the sea.

The reality is, of course, more complex. Brian was an exceptional figure who, despite coming from a relatively obscure family, rose to dominate Ireland. His major concern at Clontarf was to force the rebellious king of Leinster, Máel Mórda, to submit to him. Máel Mórda's ally Sihtric Silkbeard, the king of Dublin (see p. 117), used his connections to persuade several Vikings, including the Earl of Orkney, to fight on the Leinster side. The Earl may have been a pagan, but the other participants in the battle were at least ostensibly Christian, and almost all were Irish. Far from being expelled, the Vikings of Dublin took full advantage of the new political environment that followed Clontarf, and King Sihtric was to reign for more than twenty years after the battle, eventually outliving all the other major participants.

2.12. Depiction of the Battle of Clontarf, Ireland, which took place in 1014. Portrayed from an early date as a struggle between Irishmen and foreigners, the battle became an important symbol for Irish nationalists in the nineteenth century, particularly after the medieval text *Cogadh Gáedhel re Gallaibh* ('The War of the Irish with the Foreigners') was published with an English translation in 1867. Hugh Frazer, *Battle of Clontarf*, 1826. Oil on canvas, 170 x 254 cm.

The Vikings in Britain and Ireland

Raiding and warfare

Where did the Vikings settle?

There are three major sources of evidence for Viking settlement in Britain and Ireland – documentary, archaeological and onomastic (based on names). The quantity and quality of this evidence varies widely, both chronologically and geographically.

Documentary evidence provides a broad framework for Viking activity across Britain and Ireland, but settlement is rarely recorded in detail. Settlement in Scotland, for example, is recorded only in sagas (later medieval Icelandic narratives) and other Scandinavian sources from the late twelfth century onwards, long after the first settlements in the Northern Isles were established, probably in the ninth century. Contemporary Scottish historical sources for the Viking Age are exceptionally thin, and while they indicate a Scandinavian presence in northern Scotland, they tell us nothing about the process of settlement. The Irish annals provide a little more detail, as they record the establishment of *longphuirt* (raiding bases, see p. 27), some of which later developed into towns and the centres of small kingdoms, but again, these tell us little of the early settlement process. Welsh chronicles record raiding in Wales and the Isle of Man, but are similarly circumspect about settlement, while the *Chronicle of the Kings of Man*, the most important medieval source for that island, only begins at the end of the Viking Age.

Only in England do we have a clear historical account of the settlement process. The *Anglo-Saxon Chronicle* tells us that the 'Great Army' (see p. 26) divided in 874. One part under Halfdan, 'king of the Danes' (died 877), went to Northumbria, and in 876 he divided up the kingdom 'and they were ploughing and providing for themselves'. The

3.1. Areas of Scandinavian influence in Britain and Ireland. Based on a range of documentary, archaeological and place-name evidence, the date and extent of settlement varied from region to region.

The Vikings in Britain and Ireland

NORTH
ATLANTIC

NORTH

SEA

IRISH SEA

• Dublin

• York

• London

ENGLISH CHANNEL

Where did the Vikings settle?

41

The Vikings in Britain and Ireland

3.2. Slate 'trial-piece' from Killaloe, County Clare, Ireland. The carvings on this object show the characteristics of the Urnes-style, named after a (decorated) church in Urnes, Norway. The style was imported from Scandinavia in the eleventh and twelfth centuries. Killaloe was an important centre for the descendants of Brian Bórama, best known as the victor of Clontarf (see p. 37). Subtly modified Viking art styles became very popular among the Irish elite. L. 8.9 cm. British Museum 1858,0120.1.

other part of the army under the Viking leaders Guthrum, Oscytel and Anund went to Cambridge, and following further conflict with the West Saxons settled in East Anglia and parts of Mercia. Although nothing further is heard of Oscytel and Anund after their arrival in Cambridge, a treaty from the 880s between Guthrum and Alfred of Wessex details the border between their respective kingdoms.

The archaeological evidence for Viking rural settlement is diverse. Comparatively few small settlement sites ('farms') have been identified, and the majority of these are in Scotland. To some degree, this may be explained by processes of cultural change. In England and Ireland in particular, incomers abandoned some 'Scandinavian' traditions at an early date, living in rural settlements more or less indistinguishable from those of the native population. Individual artefacts and artistic styles (fig. 3.2) could also cross cultural and political frontiers – a 'Scandinavian' artefact does not necessarily demonstrate a Scandinavian presence at its findspot, or even in that area, and while the Vikings introduced large quantities of silver to the west and north, the practice of hoarding was in no way confined to Scandinavian groups. In the early Viking Age, furnished 'Viking' graves provide better evidence for a Viking presence, even if some isolated graves may be the product of raiding rather than settlement. The later development of distinctive 'colonial' sculptural forms in some areas points to a well-established insular Scandinavian elite, even if its dwellings cannot be identified at present.

Place-names deriving from the language of the Vikings are found in varying levels of density in parts of Britain and Ireland. Their overall distribution suggests areas of settlement, but the evidence they provide is not straightforward. Many Scandinavian words entered the languages of settled regions and became part of the 'native' naming vocabulary; conversely some place-names may have been bestowed by Viking overlords rather than evolving in the speech of inhabitants. Nevertheless, the great number and varied nature of these place-names in some areas points to a level of linguistic influence that could not have resulted from a small number of powerful individuals, but only from considerable numbers of Scandinavian-speakers (see chapter 4).

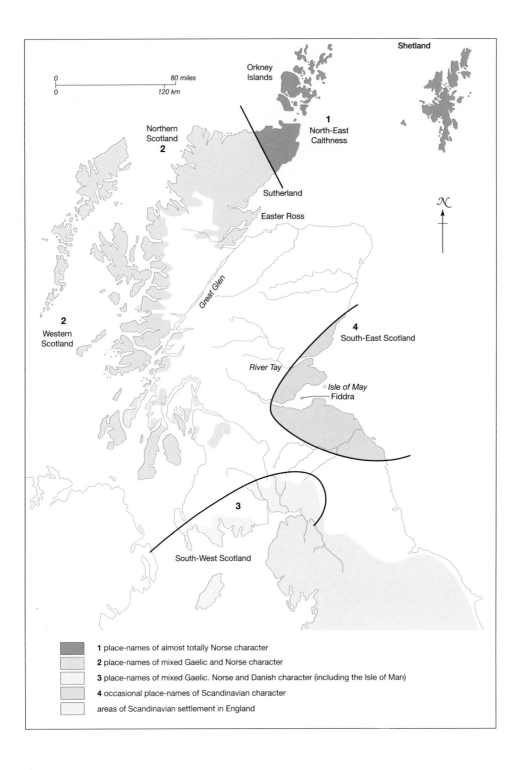

Shetland

Orkney
Islands

Northern
Scotland
2

1
North-East
Caithness

Sutherland

Easter Ross

Great Glen

2
Western
Scotland

4
South-East Scotland

River Tay

Isle of May
Fiddra

N

3

South-West Scotland

1 place-names of almost totally Norse character
2 place-names of mixed Gaelic and Norse character
3 place-names of mixed Gaelic. Norse and Danish character (including the Isle of Man)
4 occasional place-names of Scandinavian character
areas of Scandinavian settlement in England

0   80 miles
0   120 km

Scotland

The one area where rural settlement sites are readily identifiable is Scotland. Extensive settlement in Shetland and Orkney is also suggested by the linguistic evidence: the place-names are almost entirely of Scandinavian origin, and Norn, a Scandinavian-derived language, was spoken there from the Viking Age to the eighteenth century. Scandinavian did not survive so long in the Hebrides, but nevertheless Scandinavian names are to be found on all the islands, thickly scattered on Lewis and Skye, for example, and relatively sparsely further south and east. Some are found on the corresponding coastal areas of the mainland, and also in Galloway, where they form part of a continuum with the names of north-west England (fig. 3.3). In south-east Scotland, they may represent a later Anglo-Scandinavian incursion. The linguistic and archaeological evidence (particularly settlement sites and graves) is complementary and points to extensive settlement in both the north and west, with strong similarities between the two areas. Settlements are essentially confined to coastal areas and were clearly dispersed.

Most excavated farms seem to consist of at least one rectangular or sub-rectangular dwelling, often with a number of smaller, subsidiary structures nearby. 'True' longhouses, with accommodation for humans and animals under the same roof, seem to have been rare, but these were also becoming unfashionable in Scandinavia at the time. There are strong parallels between many of these houses and sites and their Norwegian equivalents, but elsewhere in Scotland individuals who used Scandinavian-style artefacts occupied or reoccupied buildings which followed very different structural traditions. This may indicate the adoption of local practices by migrant groups, or the continuing presence of native groups not otherwise attested in the archaeological or historical record. In many areas, there seems to have been a settlement hierarchy, with a number of smaller sites dependent on a larger farm situated on the best agricultural land in an area.

3.3. Place-names provide some of the best evidence for Viking settlement in Britain and Ireland. This map divides Scotland into four zones. In the north is an area where place-names remain almost entirely Scandinavian in origin. In the west is a mixture of Scandinavian and Gaelic names, and place-names of the south-west also show the influence of the Irish Sea area. Those in the east of Scotland may be relatively late. While the precise interpretation of this evidence is debated, there is a correspondence between the density of surviving place-names and Viking settlement.

Scatness – a Scottish rural site

Most research on Viking settlement in Scotland has focused on sites with rectangular houses comparable to those found in contemporary Scandinavia. These are very different to the structures built by the local inhabitants before the beginning of the Viking Age, even if they often occupy the same sites, as at Jarlshof (Shetland), Buckquoy (Orkney) and Drimore (West Hebrides). These and other sites remain important, but recent research has identified potential 'Viking' activity at sites without comparable 'Norse' houses. At Old Scatness, Shetland, an important concentration of finds and some other features have been identified within the later levels of an existing 'wheelhouse', a domestic circular stone structure, which itself forms part of a very complex multi-period site. A long hearth and a major concentration of soapstone (steatite) artefacts point to a Scandinavian presence at the wheelhouse, which was probably already derelict in the early Viking Age. Elsewhere on the site, however, the deposition of ceramic material suggests that native occupation also continued. These finds point to a complex settlement process in Scotland, with elements of continuity as well as displacement.

Vikings on the Clyde

The evidence for Viking settlement in northern and western Scotland is relatively extensive (see p. 44), but it is often not appreciated that the Vikings also left a permanent mark in southern Scotland. A number of Scandinavian place-names are recorded on either side of the River Forth, and stretching up the east coast beyond the River Tay (fig. 3.3), and the same area has several surviving stone monuments. Both stones and place-names may represent secondary settlement by Anglo-Scandinavians from north-east England.

The situation on the River Clyde is harder to interpret. There are few Scandinavian place-names in the area, and relatively few archaeological remains of the Vikings, although a small number of Viking hoards have been found in the region, and a Viking male burial recently excavated close to Loch Lomond in the highlands is the second from this area. Dumbarton Rock was also the heart of the British kingdom of Strathclyde in the west of Scotland, which covered the area around the Clyde, and extended down into Cumbria. This kingdom existed before the Viking Age, and was gradually absorbed into the emerging kingdom of the Scots in the late tenth and eleventh centuries. It is not normally seen as a 'Viking' kingdom, but the parish church at Govan Old in Glasgow contains one of the most important concentrations of insular Scandinavian sculpture anywhere in the British Isles, and is the centre of a wider network of sculptures in what is called the 'Govan style' along the Clyde (fig. 3.4). Records of a 'Doomster Hill' (destroyed by later building developments) close to the church may suggest a mound used for Viking law-assemblies, with parallels in Dublin and the Isle of Man (see pp. 122–3).

The reasons for this Scandinavian presence probably lie in a network of tenth-century alliances. Although Viking relations with the area were not always peaceful – in 870, for example, a fleet from Dublin led by the Viking leaders Olaf and Ivarr attacked Dumbarton, carrying off prisoners to be sold as slaves (see pp. 123–7) as well as loot – the tenth-century descendants of this same Ivarr, who ruled Dublin and (more intermittently) Northumbria, seem to have formed a strategic alliance with the kings of the Scots and of Strathclyde in the face of Athelstan's

3.4. Hogback tombstone from Govan Old Parish Church, Glasgow, Scotland. Hogbacks, so called for their shape, are not found either in Scandinavia or in pre-Viking Britain, but represent a new type of Viking-Age 'colonial' monument. Most are found in northern England and southern Scotland, and there is some variation in style between areas. Govan, on the River Clyde, has one of the most important concentrations, in Scotland, of hogbacks and stone crosses showing Scandinavian influence.

unification of England (see p. 29). For example, Guthfrith, king of Dublin (921–34), fled to Strathclyde in 927 after being expelled from Northumbria by Athelstan, before returning to Dublin. The kings of Dublin, Strathclyde and the Scots also fought together against Athelstan in the 930s, perhaps most notably at the Battle of Brunanburh in 937 (p. 29). The exact relationship between the different dynasties remains unclear, but Scandinavian names appear in the Scottish royal house just after this, and it is possible that a member of the Dublin dynasty was granted an estate at Govan, or that one of the rulers of Strathclyde was of partially Hiberno-Norse descent, since such a concentration of monuments points to a settlement of very high status.

England

Much of northern and eastern England saw Viking settlement. The distribution of Scandinavian-derived place-names tallies well with the boundary established in the treaty between Alfred and Guthrum (p. 43). Such place-names are largely confined to the 'Danish' side of this boundary, which tracks 'up the [River] Thames, and then up the [River] Lea, and along the Lea to its source, then in a straight line to Bedford, then up the [River] Ouse to Watling Street [an important Roman Road still in use today as the A5]'. However, the treaty tells us nothing of the boundary further north, since neither Alfred nor Guthrum had direct authority in the Midlands. Judging by both place-names and the distribution of Anglo-Scandinavian sculpture, the border of Viking settlement ran north from Watling Street to the River Trent, and then up the River Dove (more or less the border of modern Staffordshire), and then across to the Wirral in north-west England. Names ending in -by 'farm, village', -toft 'farmstead, plot of land', -wath 'ford', -beck 'stream', and -dale 'valley' are common in Scandinavian England, but they are not distributed evenly: the density is very considerable, for example, in areas of Lincolnshire and Leicestershire, but much less so in some areas of the West Riding of Yorkshire and Derbyshire, and they are largely absent from Cambridgeshire.

3.5. The Pitney Brooch. This gold Anglo-Scandinavian artefact, decorated in an eleventh-century style called 'Urnes' (see fig. 3.2), was found in a churchyard in Pitney, Somerset, England. It is by no means certain, however, that it provides evidence for a Viking community in this area, as there is little evidence for Vikings in south-west England. Diam. 3.9 cm. British Museum 1979,1101.1.

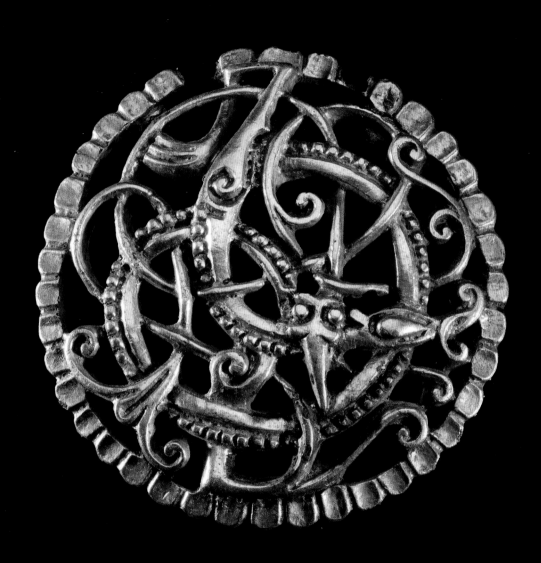

3.6. Oval copper-alloy brooch from a woman's grave in the Phoenix Park, Dublin. Brooches such as this formed part of the costume of many well-to-do Scandinavian women. This woman, whose grave contained a second oval brooch and an insular mount (fig. 2.2) could either have lived in the *longphort* at Dublin or on a small farm in its hinterland. Ninth century. L. 10.4 cm. British Museum 1854,0307.1.

The story of the West-Saxon conquest, whereby the kingdom of Wessex, the only surviving Anglo-Saxon kingdom, gained control of Viking England (p. 29), indicates that the Vikings organized themselves in territories around towns. A number of these towns can be identified, particularly in the Midlands, although fewer are recorded in East Anglia, York is the only one north of the Humber, and there are none in the north-west. By contrast, place-names, sculpture and single finds indicate a widespread presence in rural areas across north-west England, as well as Yorkshire, the East Midlands and parts of East Anglia. However, different types of evidence may suggest differences in the character of the settlement. For example, single finds of low-status Anglo-Scandinavian dress fittings are common in East Anglia, but Scandinavian place-names are comparatively less so. This may indicate that Viking settlement was less intensive than further north, but that a sense of Scandinavian identity, or even simply a taste for Scandinavian fashion, was strong.

Ireland

Settlement patterns in Ireland were very different to those in England, Scotland and elsewhere. Viking settlers in Ireland are often called 'Hiberno-Norse', a term which reflects both their Scandinavian origins and their adoption of a range of Irish customs and practices. Their activity seems to have been focused in coastal towns, with little or no rural settlement (see pp. 53–4). Place-name evidence is scanty: the names of several important settlements on the south and east coasts – Waterford, Wexford, Arklow and Wicklow – derive from Old Norse, but otherwise Scandinavian names are mostly those of islands and headlands, such as Howth ('headland') and Dalkey ('thorn island'), on either side of Dublin Bay. Nevertheless, major towns such as Dublin, Waterford and Limerick could not have survived without a hinterland to provide basic foodstuffs and other raw materials necessary for daily life. We know most about *Fine Gall*, the 'territory of the foreigners' which surrounded Dublin, but even here the evidence for Scandinavian rural settlement, as opposed to the political domination of an Irish population, is limited. An interesting exception is Cherrywood, County Dublin, where excavations have revealed a number of rectangular structures and several artefacts with strong Scandinavian associations. Away from the urban enclaves, the evidence for settlement is even more limited, but it has recently been argued that a series of small coastal 'way stations' along the sea route between Cork and Limerick, provide further evidence of Viking settlement. Beginish, in County Kerry in south-west Ireland is the only excavated example. In the north-east and on the west coast, too, isolated Viking graves may mark small coastal settlements.

Wales and the Isle of Man

Despite their geographical proximity, the evidence for Viking settlement in Wales and on Man could not be more different. In Wales, the evidence for any kind of Viking settlement rests on a handful of poorly furnished graves and a number of stray finds which may or may not have been deposited by Scandinavian settlers. Scandinavian place-names are largely confined to coastal features and island-names, but a few of the most significant settlements on the south coast have Scandinavian-derived names – Swansea 'Svein's island' and Fishguard 'fish enclosure' are two examples. Of crucial importance is the site of Llanbedrgoch, on Anglesey (itself possibly Scandinavian: 'Ǫngul's island'), a small, enclosed site a short distance from the sea which was probably occupied by a Scandinavian group at some point during its occasionally violent history (fig. 2.3). The Isle of Man, on the other hand, provides some of the best and most diverse evidence for Viking settlement anywhere in these islands. Scandinavian derived place-names are abundant, and excavations of some rural sites have revealed structures similar to those in Scotland (see p. 45). For a relatively small island, there is also a remarkable collection of dispersed Viking graves. As elsewhere, these generally isolated burials are usually associated with individual farms. Following the conversion to Christianity, the richer members of the community were buried under stone slabs, many with runic inscriptions and decoration in the

'Borre style', a type of ornamentation of Scandinavian origin which was popular in the ninth and tenth centuries (fig. 1.5). These memorials are found throughout the island, again pointing to a dispersed, rural population. Some of the inscriptions suggest a population with strong links to native as well as Scandinavian cultures.

Settlement patterns

The strong differences in evidence for Viking rural settlement across Britain and Ireland reflect genuine variations in settlement patterns. In Ireland and Wales, rural settlement seems to have been exceptionally rare, while in Scotland and on Man, the evidence suggests that it was relatively common. England is problematic: the extensive documentary and linguistic evidence for rural settlement in many areas is not matched by comparable archaeological evidence. Clearly, incoming Scandinavian groups could respond to the local environment and its existing cultures in very different ways. Not all migrant families chose to live in the kind of houses typically associated with Scandinavia, and the artefacts, structures and art styles used by Scandinavian communities in Britain and Ireland are characterized at least as much by their diversity as their common elements. While objects of Scandinavian origin were clearly valued, migrant communities also made use of local artefacts, or developed 'colonial' monuments, such as the hogback stones found from Derbyshire, England, to Scotland (fig. 3.4) and the Gosforth Cross (fig. 5.5).

The differences between regions cannot be explained chronologically. For example, while it is often assumed that northern Scotland was settled first, followed by the Western Isles and then the Irish Sea basin, this model is not sustainable. Instead, Viking groups seem to have seized certain 'key' locations, from which settlement spread outwards. There are far stronger chronological divisions between the beginnings of settlement on the east and west coasts of the Irish Sea than between Ireland and Scotland, and the essentially tenth-century land-taking of Cumbria and the Isle of Man is also markedly later than the ninth-century settlements which seem to have been typical of eastern England.

Rural life

Across these islands, rural life was influenced by local factors. Subsistence and perhaps the production of a small, tradable surplus formed the primary occupation of all but a handful of rural dwellers, but those settling in Shetland had very different lives from those in East Anglia. Climate, soil quality and the availability of resources had a profound influence on settlement. In northern Scotland, the inhabitants of many rural sites engaged in fishing, and, in time, in large-scale production of dried stock-fish. In the inland regions of England, there was almost certainly more emphasis on cereal production, although upland sites such as Ribblehead, North Yorkshire, may have focused on stock-raising. In Ireland, it seems the Vikings had little impact on a rural economy which emphasized dairying, although there is increasing evidence for cereal production, perhaps under Viking influence, and a few Old-Norse loanwords in Irish may indicate Viking-led farming innovations or developments, notably the modern Irish words for bean (*pónair*) and sheaf (*punnan*).

For those living on a conventional 'Viking' farm, life would have centred on the farmhouse, usually with a main room divided into three aisles, and with a central hearth. Diet varied from place to place as these settlements were largely self-sufficient and relied on accessible foodstuffs, but this is not to say they were necessarily isolated. Most excavated sites

3.7. Anglo-Scandinavian carved gravestone from Bibury, Gloucestershire, England. The carving is in the 'Ringerike style', named from a region of Norway, and dating from the early eleventh century, although Gloucestershire (and the south-west more generally) was not an area of significant Scandinavian settlement. H. 63.5 cm. British Museum 1913,0203.1. Donated by Rev. F.G. Dutton.

have yielded at least some imported material, pointing to wide-ranging, if sporadic, connections. At a limited number of high-status rural sites, principally in Scotland, these connections were relatively extensive.

Scale and impact

One of the great debates about ninth- and tenth-century settlement, particularly in England and Scotland, is about its scale and extent. In the Northern and Western Isles, linguistic evidence suggests it was extensive. Viking-Age finds indicate that settlement was overwhelmingly Scandinavian in character, even if limited local influences are visible at some sites. It is, of course, possible that some native inhabitants survived, perhaps adopting some elements of Norse customs and culture, but they are effectively invisible in the archaeological record. This suggests that many settlers arrived over extended periods of time, but we can have no idea of absolute numbers.

As already noted, the situation in England is even more complex, with a mismatch between sources. On the one hand, documentary and, particularly, place-name evidence, suggests considerable Scandinavian settlement. Archaeology, on the other hand, does not provide secure evidence for a substantial 'Viking' presence. This lack of archaeological evidence suggests relatively limited migration, but it could also be explained by adaptation on the part of many settlers: some members of the 'Great Army' could have been active in England for fifteen years or more before 'settling down', and they probably followed their leaders in adopting Christianity and other local practices at an early date. Nevertheless, traditional interpretations of the resulting settlement as exceptionally extensive and associated with the mass displacement of the existing Anglo-Saxon population have long since been abandoned. While some archaeologists argue for very limited settlement, other scholars, particularly linguists, believe that a small number of settlers, even if operating at an elite level, could not have had such a profound effect on the place-names and landscape organization of the northern and eastern parts of England. The reality lies somewhere between the two.

3.8. *Overleaf* Mainland, Shetland. Shetland offered good grazing land for sheep, while the land was also more fertile in the Viking Age, offering greater opportunities for arable farming than today. However, the rocky coastline and fierce tides were notoriously dangerous for ships.

Language and literacy

Old Norse, the language of the Vikings, is a northern variety of the Germanic language family, of which English, Dutch and German are also members. The earliest examples of the Germanic language used in Scandinavia take the form of runic inscriptions dating from the late second to the late fifth centuries AD (see below), but for a distinctively Scandinavian form of language – one that shows developments distinct from those of its more westerly and southerly cousins – we look to the runic inscriptions that date to about the seventh century and later. These give an impression of remarkable uniformity in language across Scandinavia during this period, although there was probably more variation between dialects than the surviving evidence indicates. During the Viking Age more clearly observable dialects developed in different places, and it is customary to divide Old East Norse, spoken in Denmark and Sweden, from Old West Norse, spoken in Norway and Iceland, although the situation was more complex than this division suggests. Varieties from all parts of Scandinavia were brought to the British Isles. Danish influence was heaviest in the eastern areas of England, and Norwegian in the north-west of England, western and northern Scotland, and on the Isle of Man and Ireland, but again the situation would not have been clear-cut – there were also Norwegians in the English East Midlands, and Danes in the Irish Sea region.

Runes

Runic characters (or runes) were used in Scandinavia from about AD 200 through to the late Middle Ages, c.1300–1500. They are made up of straight lines, which made them suitable for carving. Before about 700, a twenty-four-character set of runes (an alphabet of sorts) was used for inscriptions in the Germanic world, including Scandinavia, where the bulk of the surviving inscriptions are found. This character-set (a rune-row) is known as the Older *Fuþark* (or the futhark – the letter *þ* has the sound values of modern English 'th'), *fuþark* being the first six characters of the rune-row. There are almost four hundred surviving inscriptions which make use of it. They are found on a number of portable objects made from a variety of materials – on pieces of military kit, on gold pendants, on various personal belongings and tools, and, towards the end of their period of use and only in Scandinavia, on stone monuments. Many of the inscriptions are difficult to read, either because they are worn and only partly legible, or because they do not seem to represent meaningful words, but others may be names, possibly of the object inscribed or of individuals – those who carved the runes or who were commemorated in the act of carving – and some single-word inscriptions may have had some significance within the belief-systems of the people responsible for them.

Runes continued in use beyond the seventh century in Scandinavia, in Frisia (the modern Netherlands), and also in England where they had first appeared in the fifth century, imported by the invading Anglo-Saxon tribes. Adaptations were made to the Older Futhark in these places. In England and Frisia, the rune-row was expanded to handle the development of new vowel sounds, but across Scandinavia the number of runes was reduced, despite changes in the language which had resulted in an increase in distinct vowels and a reorganization of the consonantal system. The Younger Futhark has only sixteen characters, nine of which are 'multifunctional', standing for more than one sound. It exists in two variants, short-twig and long-branch – these terms refer to the linear formations of the characters themselves – and is the rune-row used in the Viking-Age inscriptions of mainland Scandinavia, and the one which the Vikings exported to their colonies (fig. 4.1).

4.1. The Younger Futhark. Runic characters are shown together with the corresponding letters in the Roman alphabet.

ᚠ ᚢ ᚦ ᚨ ᚱ ᚴ ᚼ ᚾ ᛁ ᛅ ᛋ ᛏ ᛒ ᛘ ᛚ ᛦ

f u þ a r k h n i a s t b m l R
    'th'

Runestones

Raised runestones are high-prestige memorials, and therefore reflect the activities of a wealthy division of Viking-Age society. Around thirty Viking-Age inscriptions in mainland Scandinavia record named individuals' activities in England – the only place in the British Isles named in the corpus. Sweden boasts the greatest number of Viking-Age runestones, and a number of these commemorate military activities, of varying degrees of success, in England. Three from Södermanland may stand as examples: Grjotgard and Einridi erected a stone in memory of their father, Gudver, who 'was west in England [and] shared payment'. A second stone tells of the less successful mission of Skerdir, who 'died in England in the retinue'. One of two runestones standing in Bjudby tells of Hefnir, the son of Thorstein, who 'went to England as a young warrior, then died grievously at home'.

A more elaborate example, from Småland, includes a eulogistic verse in *fornyrðislag*, the standard poetic metre used across the Germanic world:

He was the most	*Hann vaʀ manna*
respected of men,	*mæstr oniðingʀ,*
who lost life	*eʀ a Ænglandi*
in England.	*aldri tyndi.*

Some of the Scandinavian inscriptions explicitly relate the martial activities commemorated therein to Cnut's eleventh-century campaign in England (see p. 31). An Upplandic stone (fig. 4.2), for example, gives details of men who fought in, and were rewarded for, this campaign:

And Ulf has taken three payments in England. Tosti paid the first. Then Thorketill paid. Then Cnut paid.

'Thorketill' is Thorkell the Tall, whose activities are described in the *Anglo-Saxon Chronicle* for the entries 1009–1012, and who became Earl of East Anglia in 1017. Tosti has been identified with the Tosti described by the Icelandic historian, poet and politician Snorri Sturluson as 'the mightiest and most respected man in [Sweden] who had no rank'.

Scandinavians who died in England could be commemorated there,

4.2. Runestone from Yttergärde, Uppland, Sweden. The stone commemorates Ulf, who took three *gelds* (tribute payments – see p. 31) in England. The inscription dates to the eleventh century.

4.3. This runestone, from the parish of Maughold on the Isle of Man, was placed by a man called Hedin in memory of his daughter Hlifhild. A ship has been carved to the right of the inscription. Slate, tenth or eleventh century. H. c.81 cm. Manx National Heritage.

The Vikings in Britain and Ireland

as well as in their homeland. The stone raised in Valleberga, Skåne in Sweden, which reports that Manni and Svein 'lie in London', can profitably be read alongside a Scandinavian runic inscription on a grave-marker from St Paul's Cathedral in London, which tells us that 'Ginna (or Gina) had this stone laid with Toki'.

Other identifiably Scandinavian runic inscriptions of the Younger-Futhark type are found in Britain, in Shetland, Orkney, the Hebrides, the north-west of England, and a few, likely dating to the reign of Cnut (1016–1035) and including the St Paul's stone, in the English south-east. A very large number of inscribed stone monuments – more than thirty – are on the Isle of Man (fig. 4.3). The inscriptions on Man are most closely related to the Norwegian tradition, and many are associated with crosses – here the Scandinavian tradition of raising runestones and the 'Celtic' tradition of raising crosses and cross-slabs are combined. Most of the inscriptions broadly conform to a memorial formula found elsewhere in Scandinavia, 'X raised this cross in memory of Y', though the use of *krossi* 'cross', rather than *steinn* 'stone', is particular to the Isle of Man. Celtic personal names, such as Dufgal (*Dubgall*) and Melbrigdi (*Máel Brígde*), are found alongside Scandinavian ones, and the grammar of some of the inscriptions has been described as 'non-classical', probably reflecting changes in Old Norse which had been brought about by close contact with a Celtic language (discussed further on p. 68).

Runic inscriptions occur not only on stone, of course, but also on portable objects (fig. 4.4). All twelve Scandinavian inscriptions from Dublin are on wooden, bone, or antler artefacts. Most of these are not readily comprehensible, but two, on either side of a reused piece of wood from a bucket, are of complete Younger Futhark rune-rows. An almost complete futhark rune-row – the only example from England – is found on a late ninth- or early tenth-century brooch, found west of Penrith, Cumbria in 1989, on the flat back of its hoop (fig. 4.5).

4.4. Bone comb-case from Lincoln, England with runic inscription. The runes tell us that 'Thorfast made a good comb'. Tenth century. L. 13 cm. British Museum 1867,0320.12.

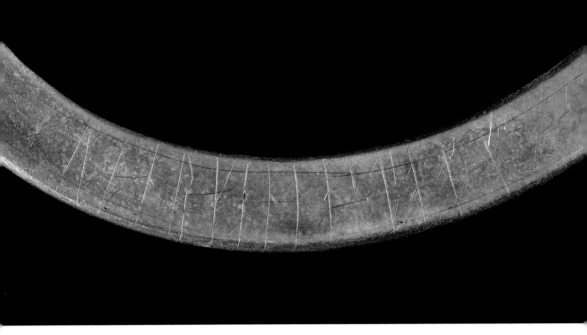

Viking poetry

Inscriptions are the only straightforwardly contemporary texts by Viking-Age Scandinavians, but certain poems may well also be genuine products of the Viking Age, despite their being preserved in Icelandic prose works of the thirteenth century and later. These poems were part of a predominantly oral culture in which verse was transmitted through speech, although some found their way on to memorial stones (as on the Småland example, p. 6o). Two main types of poetry are customarily distinguished, 'Eddic' (mostly preserved in a compendium of verse known as the *Poetic Edda*) and 'skaldic' (from Old Norse *skald*, meaning 'poet'). There are good grounds for believing that much surviving skaldic verse dates from the Viking Age. Skaldic verse is intricately structured, particularly that in *dróttkvætt* or 'court metre': alliteration and internal rhymes and half-rhymes are combined within syllable-restricted lines. Much of the vocabulary of skaldic verse belongs to a specifically poetic register, and it makes use of complex metaphors known as kennings. The characteristics of skaldic verse combine to 'fix' the text, making it resistant to change, easier to remember and therefore to transmit.

4.5. Futhark inscription on the back of one of a hoard of brooches found near Penrith in Cumbria, north-west England in 1989. The brooches are of Irish Sea origin, showing a mixture of Viking and native traditions. The area around Penrith shows evidence of Scandinavian settlement through a combination of sculpture, hoards and place-names. Silver, early tenth century. Diam. of hoop 10.4 cm. British Museum 1991,0109.2.

Later historical texts often quote skaldic stanzas as sources for the prose narrative. These are often attributed to particular poets, usually introduced with 'so says [name of poet]'. In the thirteenth century, Snorri Sturluson explicitly justifies his use of skaldic stanzas, recited before the rulers of whom he writes, as sources for his historical writing: 'the poems seem to me to be least likely to be corrupted, if they are correctly composed and judiciously interpreted'. Broadly speaking there is scholarly consensus that much of the poetry preserved in this way is indeed what it purports to be – text passed down from earlier times, largely unchanged.

The talented skald was nothing less than a sought-after and well-paid professional, welcomed by rulers in Scandinavia and elsewhere to compose poems which advertised their ancestry, valiant deeds, and wisdom. The late-thirteenth-century *Saga of Gunnlaug serpent-tongue* paints a vivid picture of the travelling skald: Gunnlaug travels from his native Iceland to London (twice), Dublin, Orkney, Skarar (Sweden), Uppsala (Sweden), and Trondheim (Norway). In these places he recites his poetry before their rulers and receives reward. In London, he praises King Ethelred II as 'England's brave prince', 'a battle-hasty ruler', and receives for it a scarlet cloak. In Dublin, Sihtric Silkbeard's battle-prowess is described in traditionally skaldic terms – he 'feeds corpses to the troll-woman's steed [wolf]' – and his generosity is pointedly praised. While Gunnlaug's saga might represent a decidedly thirteenth-century take on Viking-Age poetic practice, there is plentiful evidence to suggest that the roaming poet was a feature of Viking-Age courts in general, not least of Cnut's. *Skáldatal*, 'Enumeration of skalds', names eight individuals as Cnut's poets, and verse by six of these survives. Therein, Cnut is portrayed traditionally as a great warrior – the enigmatically-named poet, Hallvard 'Harek's-blaze' addresses him as 'shaker of the ice of the sword-belt [sword]'– but also as a Christian ruler – 'the foremost great lord under heaven', according to the poet Sigvat Thordarson.

As a Dane, Cnut may have understood the verse, but Anglo-Saxon rulers probably had greater difficulties. The *Saga of Egill Skallagrimsson* has its eponymous hero recite a *drápa*, a long formal praise poem with refrain, to English king Athelstan. The language of the poem – Old Norse – and its skaldic complexity seem not to diminish its power to please in an English

context: Egill is presented with two rings and the king's own cloak. It seems unlikely, though, that Athelstan would have been able to understand the *drápa*, if it really was recited before him. Whether he would have understood Egill's less formal utterances is a rather different question – the extent to which Old Norse and Old English were mutually intelligible is difficult to assess. The author of Gunnlaug's saga contextualizes the poet's recital in Ethelred II's court by telling his audience, 'back then, the language spoken in England was the same as that in Norway and Denmark'. While this is not precisely true, Old English and Old Norse are closely related and share much inherited vocabulary, though the two had quite different pronunciation of related words (fig. 4.6). Nevertheless there are regular correspondences between different sounds which had developed from the same origin, as can be seen below, which made possible the consistent substitution of one sound for another:

Old English	Old Norse	Modern English
stān	*steinn*	'stone'
gāt	*geit*	'goat'
stēap	*staup*	'steep'
-lēas	*-lauss*	'-less'
scip (*sc* = 'sh')	*skip*	'ship'
æsc	*askr*	'ash'
brycg (*cg* = 'dg')	*bryggja*	'bridge'
hrycg	*hryggr*	'ridge'

Old English versus Old Norse

A certain level of mutual intelligibility might well have existed between Old English and Old Norse, and the similarities between the two languages would certainly have facilitated mutual influence. English absorbed much

Scandinavian vocabulary as a result of Viking-Age language contact, and today everyday English includes many Scandinavian-derived words (egg, sky, take, leg, skirt, law, skill, etc.). Even the English pronoun system was affected: *they*, *their* and *them* undoubtedly derive from Old Norse rather than Old English, and Scandinavian influence may also have had a hand in the puzzling shift from Old English *hēo* to Modern English *she*. It is in Middle English (*c*.1100 to *c*.1500) rather than Old English manuscripts that we find texts heavily influenced by Old Norse – relatively few loanwords are on record from the Anglo-Saxon period. However, an Old English inscription on a sundial from the church at Aldbrough in the East Riding of Yorkshire gives a taste of the ways in which the everyday English of areas that saw Viking influence was inflected through contact with Scandinavian: VLF [H]ET ARŒRAN CYRICE FOR H[A]NUM & FOR GVNWARA SAVLA 'Ulf ordered the church to be raised for himself and for Gunwaru's soul'. HANVM is a form of *honum* 'him', an Old Norse pronoun in an otherwise Old English text, albeit one containing Scandinavian personal names.

On the Isle of Man, Scotland, and Ireland, Old Norse came into contact with varieties of the Celtic language family to which it is only very distantly related. There would have been no possibility of mutual intelligibility, and this goes some way towards accounting for the relative paucity of Scandinavian loanwords in these languages. In the Northern Isles and Caithness, Scotland, Old Norse completely replaced the languages spoken there, and in certain parts of the Hebridean islands, may have replaced Gaelic for five hundred years. This is evident from the very high levels of Scandinavian influence on the place-names of these areas. The place-names of Ireland, on the other hand, show comparatively little influence.

How long a Scandinavian language was spoken in various parts of the British Isles is a question which has generated much debate, and, except for those areas that saw the total displacement of their native language(s) by Old Norse, little certainty. Areas rich in Scandinavian place-names such as the English East Midlands, the Hebrides, and the Isle of Man suggest that Old Norse survived for generations after the initial period of Viking settlement, likely supported by continuing

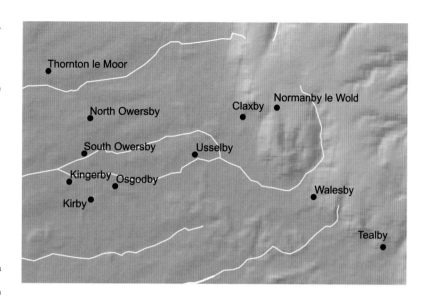

4.7. Scandinavian place-names are common in Lincolnshire, England (see also fig. 9.1). This map shows a cluster of *by*-names on the eastern edge of the Lincolnshire wolds (*by* is a common Scandinavian element meaning farm or village). In most of these names, *by* is compounded with a personal name, mostly Scandinavian (Asgautr in Osgodby, Klakkr in Claxby, Valr in Walesby), sometimes Old English (*Cynegeard* in Kingerby, *Oswald* in Usselby). The first element of Normanby is a plural form of *Norðmann* 'northman'. The people in this settlement may have been ethnically distinct from their neighbours – it has been suggested that they were Norwegians in an area of primarily Danish settlement or influence.

Scandinavian immigration to some of these areas. Runic inscriptions suggest that forms of Scandinavian were used in Britain and Ireland into the eleventh and twelfth centuries, but information about who exactly was responsible for carving them, which is necessary for a reliable assessment of their precise significance, is of course lacking.

The importance of place-name evidence to an understanding of Scandinavian activities in Britain and Ireland should by this point be clear – it has cropped up repeatedly in earlier sections. Scandinavian-derived and influenced names are often the clearest, and sometimes the only, footprints left by the speakers of Old Norse who came to these islands. As evidence they can, though, be difficult to handle. In Orkney, the Scandinavian place-name stock is relatively easily interpretable: names such as Rousay 'Hrolf's island' (ON personal name + *ey*) and Stromness 'current's headland' (ON *straumr* + *nes*) evolved in the context of a total replacement of previously-spoken languages by Old Norse. In an area such as eastern England, which apparently saw the arrival of large numbers of Scandinavian speakers but where the Norse language eventually lost out to English, the situation is far more complicated. Were Scandinavian-looking names given by speakers of Scandinavian during the Viking Age (fig. 4.7)? Or were they the product of a mixed Anglo-Scandinavian dialect, a variety rich in both English and Norse vocabulary, possibly at a much later date? Signposts sporting *by*-names may point in the direction of Britain's Viking past, but some of these names clearly belong to a post-Viking-Age naming stratum. For example, a group of *by*-names in Cumbria in England and Dumfriesshire in Scotland – including Aglionby, Robberby, and Piersby – have as their first elements personal names current in England only after the Norman Conquest of 1066.

Sometimes it is not even possible to decide whether a name contains Old English or Old Norse words – certain elements, *hūs* (OE) and *hús* (ON) (i.e. 'house') for example, are indistinguishable. Such similarities also complicate the analysis of a name like Brigsley 'clearing of/by a bridge', in Lincolnshire. The second element is Old English *lēah* 'wood, clearing in a wood', but how do we classify the first element? Its modern pronunciation reflects Old Norse *bryggja*, rather than Old English *brycg*, but are we dealing with an 'original' Scandinavian *bryggja*, or an 'original' *brycg* whose pronunciation has been affected by the area's Scandinavian(-influenced) speech, or a case of substitution of ON *bryggja* for OE *brycg*? Are such distinctions meaningless in an area in which an Anglo-Scandinavian dialect was undoubtedly developing? The name's first element is usually said to be OE *brycg* in Scandinavianized form – *bryggja* in Old Norse had the sense 'jetty' rather than 'bridge', but its usage in England could have been affected by that of its Old English equivalent. All that we can say for certain is that this name shows evidence of Scandinavian linguistic influence.

Some Scandinavian place-names preserve Old Norse inflections (grammatical endings) which operated when those names were meaningful phrases, parts of descriptive speech. The voiceless /s/ sound in the Lincolnshire name Laceby 'Leifr's farm', for example, derives from the voiceless possessive /s/ of Old Norse. The -*er*- in Witherslack 'wood's or willow-tree's hollow' (Westmorland) and Litherland '[cultivated] land on a slope' (Lancashire) derives from another distinctively Norse possessive ending, -*ar*. With these inflections, such names must have arisen in the context of Scandinavian speech – Scandinavian words could be borrowed into English and used in place-names by English speakers, but here the grammar itself is Scandinavian.

4.8. Coins provide some of the earliest surviving evidence for place-names, as they often carry the name of the town in which they were minted. The place-name De(o)raby (modern Derby), shown on this silver coin, contains the common Old Norse element -*by*, indicating Scandinavian influence. The first element is usually interpreted as a form of Old Norse *djúr* 'deer'. It may derive from an early form of Derwent, the name of the river upon which Derby sits. The name *Deoraby* appears on Anglo-Sazon coins as early as the reign of Athelstan (924–39), and again on the coinage of Edgar (959–75), shown here. Silver penny, c.973–5. Diam. 1.75 cm. British Museum BMC ii P169,8.

The Vikings in Britain and Ireland

The hammer and the cross: belief and conversion

The Scandinavians who settled in Britain and Ireland were converted, relatively rapidly in some areas, from forms of paganism to Christianity. Evidence for the belief system(s) that Christianity replaced is varied and difficult, and, in its textual form, mostly late. According to his biographer Asser, King Alfred fought against the *pagani*, and the *Anglo-Saxon Chronicle* refers repeatedly to 'heathens'; the *genti* used in Irish sources has similar connotations. Texts preserved in Iceland in the thirteenth century and later, notably the *Edda* of Snorri Sturluson and the poems of the *Poetic Edda*, paint vivid pictures of the creation of the world and of a pantheon of unruly pagan gods and goddesses who battle with giants. These texts, though, were written for particular purposes within a context that had long been Christian, and therefore may not reflect beliefs current in Viking-Age Scandinavia, or indeed in Viking-Age Britain and Ireland. Place-names across Scandinavia, for example, contain a smaller number of deity-names than are mentioned by Snorri, and their distribution suggests anything but religious homogeneity: for example Tyr, the name (according to Snorri) of Odin's one-handed son, is common in Denmark but extremely rare elsewhere.

Iconography and symbols

There are striking correspondences, however, between the stories of the later Icelandic texts and the iconography of the Viking sculpture which survives in Britain and Ireland. The story of the god Thor's fishing expedition with the giant Hymir is found in both *Gylfaginning* 'The tricking of Gylfi', the first part of Snorri's *Edda* (fig. 5.1), and in the Eddic poem *Hymiskviða*, 'The Lay of Hymir': Thor snares with an ox-head the World Serpent (*Miðgarðsormr*), which lies in the ocean, 'the girdle of all

5.1. Illustration of Thor fishing for the Midgard serpent. From an 18th-century Icelandic manuscript, Stofnun Árna Magnússon MS 66, fol. 79v.

The Vikings in Britain and Ireland

5.2. Stone cross fragment from Gosforth, Cumbria. Tenth century. This image seems to show Thor and the giant Hymir fishing for the World Serpent, a myth also recorded in later Icelandic sources (see fig. 5.1). The Gosforth Cross (see p. 76), also carved with some scenes from pagan mythology, is in the same churchyard.

5.3. Thor's hammer pendant from North Yorkshire, England. This artefact has been made from the central part of a folding balance, which has the same T-shape as other purpose-made representations of Thor's hammer. Copper-alloy. Ninth century. L. 4.4 cm. British Museum 2006,1203.16.

lands'. The extraordinary collection of Anglo-Scandinavian sculpture at St Mary's church in Gosforth, Cumbria, includes a representation of two figures in a boat, one fishing with an enormous hook (fig. 5.2). There is little doubt that here we have a picture of the Thor and Hymir episode. Sculptures found at Gosforth, Skipwith (East Riding of Yorkshire), and Ovingham (Northumberland) appear to depict certain scenes from the Battle of Ragnarok which will take place between the gods and the giants at the end of the world, as described by Snorri and in the Eddic poem, *Vǫluspá*, 'The Seeress's Prophecy'. On the east side of the Gosforth cross (fig. 5.5), a small figure holding a spear stands with his foot on the lower jaw of a beast, while his hand pushes up against the upper jaw. This is likely to be the god Vidar, slaying the wolf Fenrir to avenge its killing of Odin. A cross-shaft from Ovingham shows Fenrir swallowing the sun, and the god Heimdall with his horn, blown to summon the gods. The distribution of these scenes across Northumbria reveals the widespread currency of these pagan stories in Scandinavian England, and memorial stones at sites such as Kirk Andreas and Jurby on the Isle of Man also seem to show Ragnarok scenes. Nevertheless, these carvings occur within Christian contexts, and were probably being used to convey Christian messages. For example, the death of the gods at Ragnarok could be seen as a parallel both to the Crucifixion and to the Christian concept of Doomsday, while Thor's battles with the World Serpent could be equated with the fight against the Devil.

With the exception of these few carvings – clearly produced under strong Christian influence – there is surprisingly little archaeological evidence for pagan beliefs among Viking settlers in Britain and Ireland. As with most of Scandinavia, formal religious buildings are unknown, suggesting that ritual activity must have taken place in the home or its environs, or in outdoor places of assembly. Symbols which can readily be associated with religious belief are also rare, and it has even been suggested that amulets such as Thor's hammers (fig. 5.3) were in themselves reactions to Christianity – before encounters with Christians became a regular occurrence, there was no need for such symbols to express a 'pagan' identity that was diverse in its beliefs and expression. Amulets and talismans can also be very difficult to interpret, and were not always

5.4. Copper-alloy 'Valkyrie' mount found in Cambridgeshire, England. A number of mounts or pendants are known from both Britain and Scandinavia which show apparently female figures armed for war. This particular example is more elaborate than most, and shows a female figure on foot greeting a mounted warrior. This may well be an image of a Valkyrie welcoming a hero to Valhalla, the hall of the slain and presided over by Odin. Ninth to tenth century. H. 23.5 cm; W. 33.5 cm. British Museum 1988,0407.1.

pagan – many medieval Christian scholars, for example, credited amber with special qualities. While it is not unreasonable to suggest that small pendants in the form of female figures represent Valkyries ('Choosers of the Slain'; fig. 5.4) – female mythical figures closely associated with battle – this need not be the case, and even Thor's hammers can sometimes be interpreted as Christian Tau (T-shaped) crosses.

The Gosforth Cross

The Gosforth Cross is the best known of a number of Anglo-Scandinavian stone carvings which survive at St Mary's parish church in Gosforth, Cumbria (fig. 5.5). A little more than four metres tall, its slender profile is exaggerated by an unusually small cross-head, which is of a type often called 'Celtic', and carries patterns of geometric interlace. Part of each side of the shaft carries further interlace designs, each in a slightly different style, but mostly combining with animal-head terminals to create stylized beasts. The motifs suggest links with the broader Irish-Sea region, and particularly with the sculptural traditions of the Isle of Man, where the

5.5. The Gosforth Cross, Cumbria is an exceptional piece of Anglo-Scandinavian sculpture. The figurative scene within the round border approximately halfway up its shaft seems to depict the bound god Loki (see p. 77), and another figure on this west face may be the god Heimdall (p. 75). H. *c.* 4 m.

The Vikings in Britain and Ireland

'ring-chain' motif associated with the Scandinavian 'Borre style' (pp. 11 and 53) is relatively common.

The cross is, however, best known for its figurative sculpture. On one side of the cross, close to its base, is a scene of the crucifixion, with either the Roman soldier Stephaton or Longinus on one side, holding a sponge or spear, and either the Virgin Mary or Mary Magdalene on the other. The dress of the latter figure can be compared to that of some Valkyrie images (fig. 5.4). Elsewhere on the cross, however, are scenes from Norse mythology, including the slaying of Fenrir by Vidar at Ragnarok, and two other possible Ragnarok scenes. Later texts relate how Loki the fire-god was imprisoned by the gods for his crimes against them, bound in a cave beneath a serpent dripping venom. His release signalled the beginning of the Battle of Ragnarok. The cross seems to show the bound Loki on its west face (fig. 5.5), and further up Loki and the god Heimdall (see p. 75) may be depicted facing each other.

The juxtaposition of pagan and Christian scenes on the Gosforth Cross can be compared to the iconography of the much smaller and more damaged Thorwald's Cross on Man (fig. 5.10). Both probably reflect the period of conversion, when Norse myths with strong Christian parallels seem to have been used to illustrate Christian stories and values. The Gosforth Cross's existence also bears testimony to a wealthy patron or patrons with a keen interest in these parallels, perhaps because they themselves were relatively recent converts. Unfortunately, it does not have an inscription, so we know nothing more about its creation. Art historians date it to the tenth century, soon after Norse settlement began in this area, and, it would seem, soon after their conversion.

Burial practices

Some of the best evidence for Viking belief systems comes from burials and particularly from furnished graves, but these were as much political as religious statements, intended to reinforce the authority of the deceased's heirs. Some recent work has, however, pointed to the potentially religious or magical aspects of a number of different grave-goods, including whalebone plaques that may have links to the veneration or invocation of the fertility goddess Freyja (fig. 5.6) and iron staffs or 'wands' (fig. 5.7). Many of these objects were placed in the graves of women, and later literary sources also emphasize the feminine aspects of magic-working and some other ritual activities.

Viking burial practices were diverse. The most characteristic (or, rather, the most archaeologically visible) is the deposition of grave-goods, typically weapons with men (fig. 5.8) and oval brooches with women (figs 3.6 and 5.9), but by no means all 'Viking' furnished graves include gender-specific artefacts. Other objects placed in these graves include a wide range of dress-fasteners, and more rarely tools associated with metal-working or textile production. Objects of insular origin, including brooches, pins, buckles and strap-ends, are also relatively common. In Britain and Ireland, most furnished burials are found in the north and west, with distinct concentrations in areas such as Dublin and Orkney, which were important power centres at the time. Across much of Viking England, on the other hand, this practice was very rare. Recent excavations at Heath Wood, Derbyshire, have identified an important cremation cemetery with relatively modest grave-good assemblages. Each cremation was marked by a low mound. These features also occur at some other 'pagan' burial sites. Apart from Heath Wood, however, cremation was very rare, and most Viking communities practiced inhumation (burial without burning).

Elsewhere in England and in parts of Scotland, high-status Scandinavian graves were marked with elaborate stone monuments, particularly 'hogback' stones (fig. 3.4). These represent an adaptation of an existing Anglo-Saxon monument tradition which marked important burials with elaborately carved recumbent (flat) stones. On the Isle of

5.6. Whalebone plaque, from Lilleberge, Norway. Ninth century. These artefacts are usually found in well-furnished women's graves, and are often interpreted as 'ironing boards'. More recently, it has been suggested that they are linked to the veneration of the fertility goddess Freyja. Whatever their precise ritual associations, these exceptionally well-crafted objects were clearly symbols of status closely associated with women. H. 23 cm. British Museum 1891,1021.67.

5.7. Iron staff or 'wand' from Vestnes, Romsdalfjord, Norway, late ninth to tenth century. Traditionally interpreted as roasting spits, recent research has suggested that they may instead have been associated with a type of magic-working called *seiðr*. This example is unusual in being deliberately bent: this ritual activity is normally confined to weapons. At least two of these staffs (or wands) have been found in the British Isles. L. (following the curve) 90 cm. British Museum 1894,1105.5.

Man, the sculptural tradition is slightly different, and often includes runic inscriptions in Old Norse (figs 4.3 and 5.10). It should be noted that across Britain and Ireland these two burial practices – furnished graves and the use of carved stone grave-markers – were mutually exclusive, and it is rare even to find them at the same sites.

All of these funerary practices seem to have been restricted to the upper levels of Scandinavian society, and it is likely that they served as powerful statements of new socio-political realities. In the absence of other evidence, it must be assumed that the majority of the Viking population were buried in unfurnished graves which are effectively indistinguishable from those of the native population. Certainly, they cannot be securely identified at present.

5.8. Reconstruction of a Viking grave from Eyrephort, County Galway, Ireland, found in 1947. This male burial was accompanied by a sword, spear and shield, only the boss of which survives. It seems likely that it was associated with a small settlement on the west coast of Ireland. Drawing by P. Johnson.

The Barra burial

In September 1862, an exceptionally well-furnished Viking grave was found at Ardvouray, on the west coast of Barra, in the Western Isles of Scotland. The burial site was marked with a standing stone and the body was accompanied by a pair of oval brooches, a ringed-pin, an iron buckle, a comb, a drinking horn (of which only the mounts survive), a knife, a whetstone, and three tools associated with cloth production – a heckle or carding comb (used for teasing flax stems or wool into thread), a weaving sword and a pair of shears (fig. 5.9).

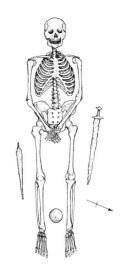

The Vikings in Britain and Ireland

Although the skeletal material has been lost, the oval brooches suggest that this was the grave of a woman, who was buried dressed in clothing which reflected a Scandinavian identity. The ringed pin and perhaps the drinking horn mounts, on the other hand, point to more local, insular associations. It seems likely that the associated standing stone predated the burial, and that the woman's community consciously chose to associate her grave with a more ancient (and local) past.

Furnished women's graves are more common in Scotland than elsewhere in the British Isles, but the Barra burial is particularly rich, at least by insular standards. Knives are relatively common finds in Viking-Age graves, but perforated whetstones are rarer. Textile-working tools are rarer again, particularly in any quantity. Their presence in this grave reflects the importance of the various processes associated with cloth production in this period, and they can be compared to the whalebone plaques found in other women's graves (fig. 5.6). All were presumably seen as status symbols equivalent to the smithing tools which sometimes accompanied contemporary male furnished graves. The Barra burial provides secure evidence for a relatively wealthy, rural community who settled on the west coast of the island in the ninth century, and who had not yet adopted local burial practices or beliefs.

5.9. Grave-goods from Barra in the Western Isles of Scotland. The oval brooches at the bottom corners of this image are typical finds from women's graves across the Viking world. The ringed pin and iron buckle (top right) are more typical of insular contexts. This burial was also accompanied by a comb and a whetstone (bottom) and a drinking horn, represented by a set of copper-alloy mounts (left and right). The large iron object is the remains of a heckle. The grave also produced some small copper-alloy objects, a knife, a weaving sword and a pair of shears (not shown in this picture). British Museum 1895,0613.1–13.

5.10. Thorwald's Cross, Kirk Andreas, Isle of Man, tenth century. This striking, if badly damaged cross-slab shows on one face (left) an image of the Norse god Odin, holding a spear and accompanied by a raven, being devoured by the wolf Fenrir, a scene from Ragnarok, the end of the world in Old Norse mythology. On the opposite face of the cross (right), a figure holding a book and cross, presumably a saint, tramples a serpent. The fish carved beside this figure must be a symbol of Christianity. The symbolic relationship between these two scenes remains the subject of debate. H. 36.5 cm; W. 19.5 cm. Manx National Heritage.

Christianity versus paganism

Religious interaction between the Vikings and the inhabitants of Britain and Ireland is often seen as a violent conflict between Christian natives on the one hand and 'pagan' or 'heathen' Vikings on the other. The latter terms are taken directly from contemporary historical sources, but these accounts were written by Christian churchmen, and coloured by the fact that Vikings raided and even destroyed Christian churches. There was more flexibility from both sides than such a simple picture suggests. It was easy for the Vikings to accept one more god alongside

The Vikings in Britain and Ireland

the many whom they already recognized, while Christianity had a long history of assimilating the sacred places, festivals and even gods and goddesses of other beliefs in order to secure long-term conversion.

This seems to have been the case in Viking Britain, as shown by the stone carvings from northern England and the Isle of Man which harness 'pagan' iconography for Christian purposes (see pp. 73–7), and by coin-evidence, which may suggest attempts to link particular Norse gods with appropriate Christian saints. Coins minted in York in the 920s carried the name of St Peter, but included both a Viking sword and the hammer symbol of Thor. In their respective belief systems, Peter was a fisherman, while Thor fished both for the god Loki and the World Serpent (fig. 5.1). The hammer perhaps suggests another parallel. Thor with his hammer defended the gods against their enemies the giants, while Peter at Gethsemane defended Christ against his enemies with a sword. Perhaps these coins were intended to convey the message that Peter was a saint that even a Viking warrior could respect.

It seems very unlikely that any Scandinavian migrant could have been entirely unaware of Christianity, whatever his or her attitude to this 'new' faith. Christian – or at least native – influences crept into what are usually thought of as 'pagan' burial practices from a very early date, perhaps most obviously in the almost total abandonment of the practice of cremation, which was frowned on by the Church at the time. The regular re-use of Christian burial sites for furnished burials does not necessarily indicate a process of conversion – instead these graveyards may have been used because they were existing burial sites associated with a displaced indigenous elite. Stone memorials within these graveyards, on the other hand, almost certainly commemorate Christians (fig. 5.2), although some of the more pagan elements of their iconography suggest that this conversion may have been relatively recent (fig. 5.10).

Textual evidence for conversion is scarce, although there is some for the Scandinavians in England. The *Anglo-Saxon Chronicle* records the conversion of the Viking leader Guthrum, following his defeat by King Alfred in 878 (p. 26). Almost all the available evidence points to a rapid conversion of those settling in England at or soon after this point, with the possible exception of Cumbria. While the churches of northern and eastern England seem to have suffered considerably in the early years of the invasion, many survived and others were founded and endowed by Anglo-Scandinavian patrons. Almost all the ecclesiastical sites in the environs of Dublin survived the Viking Age more or less intact, although the Irish annals do not formally record the conversion of the Hiberno-Norse rulers at all. This may have been because their conversion occurred in England or elsewhere in the Viking world. The first undeniably Christian king of Dublin died in retirement at the monastery of Iona in the Inner Hebrides, off the western coast of Scotland, in 980, and a bishopric was finally established at Dublin *c*.1030. A bishopric was established in Orkney a decade or two later. Some of the most interesting evidence for the conversion of the islands comes from the early thirteenth-century *Orkneyinga saga* (see also pp. 118–9). Among other key elements it describes the martyrdom of Earl Magnus of Orkney, a man of Scandinavian descent, *c*.1117. The twelfth-century cathedral at Kirkwall (fig. 5.11) was dedicated to him following his canonization in 1135. By this time, all of the Viking communities in Britain and Ireland – and indeed in Norway and Denmark – had been Christian for many generations.

5.11. St Magnus Cathedral, Kirkwall, Orkney. This magnificent structure shows strong Romanesque influences and demonstrates that despite the apparent isolation of the Earldom, Orkney was in regular contact with the wider Christian world at this time. By the time it was built, Orkney had been at least nominally Christian for well over a century.

The Vikings in Britain and Ireland

The hammer and the cross: belief and conversion

Town life

In Ireland, and to a lesser extent England, Viking settlers are now perhaps best known as the founders and promoters of towns. It is only relatively recently, however, that we have become aware of this aspect of their legacy. Until the 1970s when major urban excavations began, most notably at York in England, and Dublin and Waterford in Ireland, there was a tendency to dismiss these sites as relatively minor military bases or administrative centres.

Towns, and particularly medieval towns, have traditionally been defined legally as places distinct from the surrounding countryside that enjoyed some degree of self-government, albeit under the authority of a king or greater magnate. Because these attributes are usually identified in charters and similar legal documents, it was once assumed that towns themselves were confined to those parts of medieval Europe that produced this documentation. We know now that towns developed in many other areas, particularly in the tenth and eleventh centuries, and that more complex definitions are therefore required.

Most commentators would still argue that towns have a distinct identity in some way related to a substantial concentrated population – although 'substantial' can mean different things in different areas at different times. More important, however, is the fact that towns had complex economies. In an age when the overwhelming majority of the population worked the land, a key characteristic of any urban site was the fact that most of its population engaged in non-agricultural activities. These could include administration (either lay or clerical), large-scale production of a range of artefacts, trade – particularly over long distances – and perhaps the provision of basic services to the surrounding area.

It is often difficult to apply this definition of a town to specific sites, and the precise distinction between a major non-urban site, such as a royal manor or wealthy monastery, and a 'true' town remains open to debate. A large number of Viking settlements may have started out with a limited number of the functions of a town but very few became fully urban. Attempts to produce absolute definitions of urban status, perhaps by using a list of 'urban' characteristics, have not always met with success, and in reality, dividing lines between different levels of urbanization would have been meaningless in the Viking Age.

The first towns

Across northern Europe, the end of the Roman Empire is closely associated with the collapse of urban life. Scotland and Ireland had never been subject to Roman urbanization, but they, like those parts of northern Europe that had been under Roman rule, must also have experienced a sharp reduction in trade at this time – although there is some evidence for ongoing long-distance exchange from the fifth to the seventh centuries. The centuries before the beginning of the Viking Age saw some recovery, with the development of *emporia*, sites with limited permanent populations which nonetheless acted as centres for long-distance trade. In Anglo-Saxon England, trading sites known as *wīc*s (Old English, derived from the Latin *vīcus*, meaning a site with a commercial function) at places such as Ipswich, Southampton and London, were slightly larger but had similar functions. While there is no secure evidence for similar sites in Ireland, it is possible that some of the larger monastic sites such as Clonmacnoise (fig. 2.1), Kildare, and Armagh may also have taken on some urban characteristics. A similar case has been made for some ecclesiastical sites in England, but the character and, indeed, existence of the Irish 'monastic town' has been hotly disputed in recent years. Ironically, the best evidence dates from the Viking Age itself, when many major monasteries seem to have profited from a close association with the coastal Hiberno-Norse towns.

It is important to realize that there were few, if any, urban sites in Scandinavia at the beginning of the Viking Age, and that Viking settlers did not arrive with clearly-conceived ideas of urbanization. Indeed, some areas that saw substantial Viking settlement, such as Iceland, never saw the development of towns. Where towns did occur, they developed more or less simultaneously across the Viking world, from Russia to Ireland. Two of the earliest Scandinavian towns – Ribe and Hedeby (Haithabu in German) – developed in Denmark, while Sweden had the major urban site of Birka and Norway had Kaupang. There is clear evidence that Hedeby, at least, was a deliberate royal foundation, and the other sites, like all towns in this period, must have enjoyed royal support and protection. While there were also other smaller trading sites, it would seem that in Scandinavia, as elsewhere in the Viking world, the number of 'true' towns engaging in international trade was always relatively small.

Viking towns in England and Ireland

The distribution of Viking towns across Britain and Ireland is very uneven. While Scotland almost certainly had some 'beach markets' or small trading sites, no towns developed there in the Viking Age. Similarly, the Isle of Man, while an important power centre which has recently produced some evidence of Viking-Age beach markets, has not yet provided clear evidence of urban development in this period. Cumbria and Lancashire in England had no towns either, and Anglo-Saxon Chester, (re)founded in the early tenth century, was the most important urban centre in the area from then until the end of the Viking Age and indeed later.

Several important urban centres developed in Viking England, but again their distribution was rather uneven. In East Anglia, it seems that established Anglo-Saxon trading centres continued to function, or experienced only a short disruption at the time of the initial Viking settlement. Eastern Mercia, on the other hand, saw the development of Derby, Leicester, Lincoln, Nottingham and Stamford, sometimes referred to as the 'Five Boroughs'. Unfortunately, we know very little about urban development at most of these sites, particularly during the relatively brief period when they were under direct Viking control.

6.1. Silver pennies from Viking England. Several of the Viking towns re-used or adapted existing settlements, some of which had been towns in Roman times, and preserved all or part of their defences. The coins here, both minted between 921 and 927, name towns in England – York (left) and Lincoln (right) – using corrupted versions of their Latin names. Diam. 1.9 cm and 2 cm respectively. British Museum 1915,0507.772 and 2009,4133.670.

By the far the best English evidence comes from York, which documentary sources also suggest was the largest, richest and most important of the English Viking towns. Anglo-Saxon royal and commercial centres already existed at this important Roman site, but it was only during the Viking Age that the settlement became an important town, densely settled, with extensive manufacturing activity and wide-ranging trading contacts.

York and the other Anglo-Scandinavian towns lay at the heart of extensive territories that were subject to the same rulers, usually Viking or of Scandinavian descent, at least until the (re)conquests of the tenth century. In Ireland, Viking control was confined to a series of small enclaves, each focused on a particular urban site, but the political and economic influence of these towns extended far beyond their boundaries. The largest, richest and most important of these was Dublin, one of the few *longphuirt* (see pp. 27–9) to develop into an urban site. There is also good documentary and archaeological evidence for the Viking town of Waterford, on the south coast. Documentary evidence suggests that by the end of the Viking Age, Limerick was also an important town, although archaeological evidence for urbanization there remains limited. Wexford and Cork, on the other hand, seem to have been relatively minor sites throughout the Viking Age.

Town life

Dublin and York were by far the most important Viking towns in Britain and Ireland, and indeed in the Viking west, but debate about their relative wealth and political influence continues. A number of kings of Dublin subsequently became kings of Northumbria, with their power centre at York – a process that suggests that York was seen as a richer prize, but also that Dublin cannot have lagged too far behind.

Street-names in York

The city of York's Viking legacy is clearly visible today in the names of its streets, most obviously in the number which end in *-gate* 'road, street' (Old Norse *gata*). Near the minster we find Gillygate, Jubbergate, Goodramgate, Back Swinegate, Deangate, and so on. Medieval names which no longer exist provide further evidence of *-gate*-names – parts of the surviving Shambles (a place where meat was sold), for example, were called *Haymongeregate* and *Nedlergate* (in documents of 1240 and 1394 respectively) and a number of surviving medieval names show the replacement of *-gate* with other elements – Blossom Street was once *Ploxwangate* (1241). Medieval records also preserve further Old Norse words for lane or street which are not preserved in York's modern street names. *Geil* 'alley, narrow lane', for example, was once a common element in street-names, found in early forms of Feasegate, Spen Lane, and Fetter Lane.

When these streets gained their names, the Old Norse elements *gata* and *geil* were used in preference to existing English words, such as lane and street, which predominate in other English towns. This is strong evidence of the lasting Scandinavian influence on the everyday language of the city, but it is a far trickier business deciding which of these names might have arisen in Old Norse conversation during England's Viking Age. Some of them most certainly did not: Deangate, for example, dates to the early twentieth century. Others, though, are recorded relatively early and appear entirely Old Norse in origin, and these may be Viking-Age products, offering valuable clues to the city's development, its dwellers and its trades.

Names can tell us about both individuals and groups living in Viking-Age York. Goodramgate preserves an Old Norse personal name, either Gudrun (feminine), which would raise interesting questions about the profile of women in the city, or Guthrum (masculine). King's Court, traditionally interpreted as the seat of the Viking kings of York, derives in part from Old Norse *konungr* 'king', and its early spellings are forms of Old Norse *konungs-garðr* 'king's enclosure'. Jubbergate's early forms show that the modern name contains three elements: the thirteenth-century form Bret(t)egate suggests that the 'original' first element derived from Old Norse *Bretar* 'Britons'. This indicates that an ethnically distinctive group of people was in some way associated with this street at the time the name was coined. These 'Britons' may have been recent arrivals from Cumbria, perhaps accompanying Scandinavian-speakers, or may have remained for generations identifiably distinct from the city's other inhabitants. (A prefix, Middle English *Jewe* 'Jew', accounts for *Ju-*.)

A number of Old Norse-derived names suggest economic activity. Bootham, from Old Norse *búðum* 'at the booths', is evidence for an early marketing site, and Coppergate, Skeldergate, and Blossom Street each appear to have as their first element an Old Norse occupational term: *koppari* 'cup-maker, joiner'; *skjaldari* 'shield-maker'; and *plóg-sveinn* 'ploughman'. Blossom Street is an excellent example for demonstrating the importance of early spellings in determining a name's origin: *Ploxwangate* (1241) and *Plouswayngate* (1276) point to Old Norse *plógsveinn* ('blossom' is a later substitution based on sound-similarity).

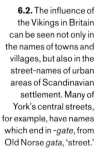

6.2. The influence of the Vikings in Britain can be seen not only in the names of towns and villages, but also in the street-names of urban areas of Scandinavian settlement. Many of York's central streets, for example, have names which end in -*gate*, from Old Norse *gata*, 'street.'

Town layout and housing

To the modern eye, Viking towns seem to provide little evidence of sustained planning, with the most obvious exception being their defences (see p. 95). Their irregular streets usually follow features of the local landscape, such as the natural ridge on which Dublin is built, or the new bridge and old (Roman) gates of York. Appearances can be deceptive, though. However irregular the streets, they were usually lined with long, narrow property plots set more or less at right angles to the direction of the street. In parts of York, the length of street frontages is so regular as to suggest they were laid out in a single event. The plots at Fishamble Street, Dublin were less regular, but property boundaries were clearly respected and reinforced from generation to generation – something which suggests an overarching authority within the town (fig. 6.3).

Occasionally, plot boundaries could be swept away and streetscapes could be reconfigured to suit new conditions. At Upper Exchange Street, Dublin, the early tenth century saw the development of industrial activity, primarily metal-working, which expanded into an area previously given over to domestic occupation, and this activity continued for the rest of the Viking Age. At Fishamble Street, on the other hand, a distinct shift in property divisions can be related to the construction of a new waterfront embankment. On the whole buildings specifically designed for industrial activity were rare. Instead, most manufacturing seems to have taken place outdoors, or in some cases within the main, predominantly domestic, structure on each plot.

Within each plot, owners or tenants clearly had considerable freedom to build as they chose, but the types of houses constructed in each Viking town are remarkably consistent, with little architectural variation. House sizes, however, varied considerably and presumably reflected the wealth of the plot owner. The largest structure on each property normally fronted the street, with smaller, subsidiary buildings in the yard behind. Occasionally, whole series of buildings could be rebuilt simultaneously, as was the case at Coppergate, York in AD 973.

At Coppergate before this date, and in the Hiberno-Norse towns throughout the Viking Age, the dominant house-type was rectangular

6.3. Reconstruction of a group of houses based on evidence from Fishamble Street, Dublin. Excavated between 1976 and 1980, this area around Wood Quay has produced some of the best evidence for Viking-Age urban life anywhere in Ireland or Britain. Up to fourteen property plots extended back from the street, some of which saw the construction of as many as thirteen successive buildings over a period of more than two hundred years. Drawing by M. Heffernan.

with post-and-wattle walls, made by weaving thin wooden rods between uprights driven into the ground (fig. 6.4). Inside, life must have revolved around the central hearths, used for cooking but also providing some light to the windowless interiors of these structures. Privacy was not a priority, with each house consisting of a single room, albeit usually divided into three aisles. Raised areas on each side of the hearth were presumably used for sitting during the day and sleeping at night.

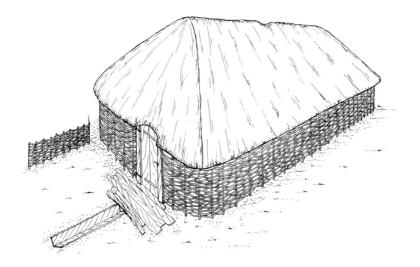

6.4. Reconstruction of a post-and-wattle thatched house from Dublin. These structures dominated Viking-Age Dublin and Waterford. Usually the largest buildings on narrow property plots, doors were placed in the end walls. These structures are closely associated with areas of Hiberno-Norse settlement and influence, but comparable post-and-wattle buildings dating to the early Viking period have also been found in York. Drawing by M. Heffernan.

At some urban sites, notably at Coppergate and Hungate, these houses were replaced by sunken-featured structures with cellars excavated beneath timber-built buildings (fig. 6.5). It is thought that these were merchants' houses, with the cellars used as secure storage areas. Several examples have also been found at Waterford in Ireland, and indeed in several Anglo-Saxon towns. Because their (wooden) floors are missing, we cannot be certain how the domestic space was arranged. Elsewhere, however, post-and-wattle houses continued to be built until the end of the Viking Age.

Whatever the house type, the plots behind each one were riddled with rubbish pits, but it is important to realize that only one or two of these pits would have been open at any one time. Their contents provide valuable evidence for the daily life of those occupying these houses, particularly for their diet.

With a few exceptions, town dwellers were reliant on food brought into their settlements from the surrounding hinterland. In Dublin, oats seem to have been predominant, perhaps eaten as a pottage, while beef was the most common meat consumed. Fish and fowl were less common, and there is rarer evidence for more luxurious foodstuffs, such as imported walnuts. Comparable evidence has been recovered at Waterford and York.

6.5. A sunken-featured building under excavation at Hungate, York. Dating from the tenth century, the wooden walls of the cellar are clearly visible, but all traces of the superstructure are gone. Usually interpreted as merchants' houses, several examples have been found at Waterford, as well as at other urban sites in Anglo-Saxon England.

Defences

Defences are one aspect of Viking towns which show clear evidence of planning. Most were situated at naturally defensive sites, at the angles between two rivers, as was the case with Dublin or Waterford, or within the remains of Roman walls, as was the case with York and Lincoln. The Hiberno-Norse defences needed to be constructed from scratch. At both Dublin and Waterford, a series of earthen banks topped by wooden palisades (or fences) were constructed, a process which culminated in stone walls – those at Dublin dating from the second half of the eleventh century, and those at Waterford built perhaps fifty years later. By the early twelfth century, the *dún* or 'fort' of Dublin was viewed as one of the wonders of Ireland. At York, the townsfolk took advantage of the existing Roman defences, but they added to these, and altered their layout to suit their own needs.

Production and trade

A key aspect of all towns is the fact that most of the population engage in non-agricultural activities, and in the Viking Age, the urban economy was dominated by production and trade, both of which occurred on a substantial scale. The two were closely linked in that urban craftsmen relied on raw materials which were invariably acquired outside the towns themselves. It is generally assumed that these materials were traded, but it is possible that other exchange mechanisms were used, particularly at local levels. Townsfolk may have acquired raw materials from land they owned or rented in the countryside, for example, or local rulers may have directed the proceeds of rents or taxes 'in kind' to these urban centres. The exceptionally good preservation conditions often associated with urban sites have enabled the recovery of an unusually wide range of materials, from which we can learn a great deal about the Vikings' trading activities, and urban economies at the time.

Many craftsmen seem to have specialized in the large-scale manufacturing of relatively low-value artefacts. At Dublin, for example, there is good evidence for specialist comb-manufacture, as well as the production of a range of bone and antler pins. Similar evidence has also been found at York (fig. 6.6) and Lincoln (fig. 4.4). At York, there is evidence for wood-turning and the production of bowls and other utensils. All of the Viking towns were essentially 'wooden worlds', and

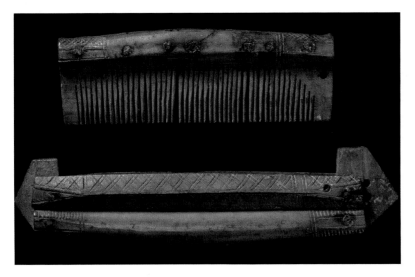

6.6. Viking-Age comb and comb case from York, England, tenth to eleventh century. Made of antler plates riveted together and decorated with some incised patterns, combs like this were common artefacts throughout the Viking Age. Comb cases were constructed in a similar way, but seem to have been rarer. L. of comb 10 cm; L. of case 14 cm. British Museum 1866,0510.1. Donated by N.W.J. Westlake.

The Vikings in Britain and Ireland

there is widespread evidence for the manufacture of other wooden objects. Leather was also worked extensively (fig. 6.7), although it was probably tanned elsewhere. While bone, antler, leather and wood could all be sourced locally, other craftsmen worked material which had travelled much greater distances. The metals used to produce the ringed-pins which are so characteristic of Hiberno-Norse groups (fig. 6.8) must have travelled a considerable distance, although we are not entirely sure where the Vikings acquired either copper or tin. Amber, on the other hand, almost certainly came from the Baltic, and was imported to both Dublin and York, where specialist workshops have been excavated. Fragments of silk found at both towns had travelled even further, the closest source being the Byzantine world, but these garments were presumably cut and sewn locally. As well as raw materials and foodstuffs, manufactured objects were also traded. Some of the best evidence comes from England, where pottery was produced in large quantities and transported over considerable distances, and the distribution of vessels is relatively easy to map. In Viking-Age Ireland and Scotland, on the other hand, pottery was largely unknown, and we know much less about local and regional trade in these areas. At the apex of the Viking trading network, however, was long-distance trade, which connected the Viking towns of Britain and Ireland to the wider Viking world, and indeed to areas where the Vikings never settled. Viking trading ships were theoretically large enough to transport large quantities of low-value materials over considerable distances, but direct archaeological evidence for this is limited. Small, valuable and exceptionally well-crafted items from distant countries are more archaeologically visible and were clearly much sought-after by elite groups inside and outside the Viking towns.

Trade and treasures

Interpretations of the Viking Age have sometimes created a strong contrast between 'raiding' and 'trading'. The distinction between the two may not always have been so clear. Trade certainly took place throughout the Viking Age, and in fact the apparent ease with which the Vikings selected wealthy churches and trading centres as targets may well have been based on familiarity gained while trading. But trading was not necessarily entirely peaceful. An argument during a supposedly peaceful trading meeting which turned violent could transform trading into raiding, and an individual might choose to raid or trade depending on circumstances. Indeed, some trading commodities may themselves have entered the market as a result of raiding or military activity. Historical sources reveal that there was an extensive trade in slaves, and fresh supplies were probably derived in part from raiding.

What linked raiding and trading was the pursuit of wealth. The ultimate measure of wealth was probably the possession of land, which was almost certainly a factor in the permanent settlement of parts of Britain and Ireland. Wealth could also be measured through ownership of livestock, by the maintenance of large households and lavish lifestyles, and through the ownership and display of precious objects, either in public or in the household. In the Scandinavian homelands, which had few major trading centres and very little evidence for the use of precious metal at the beginning of the Viking Age, gold and silver were valued primarily for their use in high-status display items, such as personal ornaments and weapon-fittings. The demand for such items in turn created demand for gold and silver as raw materials, which was met in part through Anglo-Saxon, Frankish and Islamic coins, whether these were acquired peacefully or not. This desire for gold and silver was probably a major factor in the early Viking expansion, before attention turned to permanent settlement.

The Vikings in Britain and Ireland

The taste for ostentatious personal display did not change when the Vikings settled in Britain and Ireland, not least because the native elites also had a taste for gold and silver ornaments. New styles of ornament developed as a result of the combination of Viking and native tastes, including distinctive types of brooches and arm-rings. These included kite-shaped brooches with exceptionally long pins in Ireland and, around the Irish Sea, so-called 'ball brooches' and 'bossed penannular brooches' – penannular meaning an almost complete ring. The largest examples would certainly have provided powerful visual statements of the owners' status, but were highly impractical, since they were too heavy to wear either comfortably or safely, with weights of over 600 g, and projecting pins which could exceed 50 cm in length (fig. 7.1).

7.1. Large silver brooch from near Penrith, Cumbria. While this 'ball' or 'thistle' brooch is splendid, it is too large and heavy to be practical. Early tenth century. L. 51.1 cm. British Museum 1909,0624.2.

7.2. Fragments of jet/lignite ornaments found in Dublin. Jet from Yorkshire, England has been found throughout the Viking world. As with amber, jet and lignite (which is closely related to jet) were often traded as a raw materials and worked into artefacts, particularly bracelets and rings (as shown here), at distant sites. National Museum of Ireland.

The pursuit of wealth and status also generated trade, over both long and short distances. On the one hand, trade enabled the movement of luxuries which helped to display the status of wealthy individuals within society. On the other, the profits to be derived from trade were themselves a source of wealth. Regional differences meant that different resources were distributed around the Viking world, and long-distance trade included not just finished items, but also raw materials for making them. Excavations at Dublin, for example, have revealed amber (probably from the Baltic), jet (probably from eastern England) (fig. 7.2) and whalebone (probably from Norway and the North Atlantic). Steatite, or soapstone, was used in Norway to make vessels for cooking and eating, and was also mined for the same purpose in Shetland. Such soapstone vessels were traded around the Viking world. By contrast, the Vikings in England quickly adapted to the use of pottery, and settlements in Lincolnshire such as Stamford and Torksey became centres for the large-scale production and trade of such vessels.

Trade connected Britain and Ireland to the far end of the Viking world (fig. 7.3). In addition to Islamic and Byzantine coins received in return for items traded by the Vikings themselves (including furs, falcons, amber, honey and slaves), the eastern trade route brought access to luxuries such as silk, which at this point was only being produced in Asia and around the eastern Mediterranean. Silk has been found in both Dublin and York, and the contexts of these finds suggest that its use was not restricted to the highest level of society.

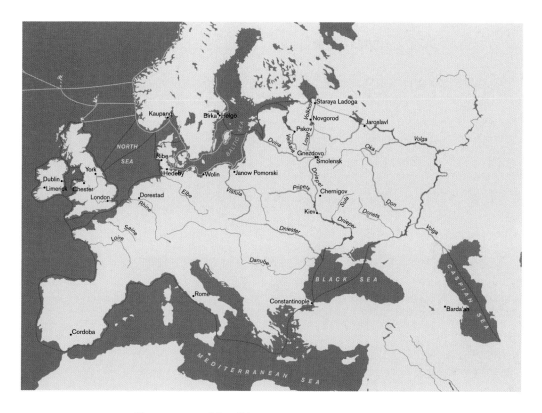

7.3. Trade routes in the Viking Age.

Barter and bullion

Many different types of payment were used in trade. These included the direct exchange of one type of trade goods for another (barter), and probably also the use of some types of easily measured commodities, including textiles, beads and furs, as means of exchange. However, the most widespread form of exchange appears to have been bullion. This is metal valued by weight rather than by a nominal face value. Bullion could take many different forms, and its use among Viking groups was probably inspired by contact with coin-using cultures. Evidence for bullion use increases from the mid ninth century, a period during which Islamic dirhams began to enter Scandinavia in large numbers, and in which there is historical evidence for large scale raiding in the coin-using

Anglo-Saxon and Frankish kingdoms. The bullion economy developing in the Viking homelands was then transferred to Viking areas of Britain and Ireland, and evidence of bullion use has been found in most areas of Viking settlement on these islands.

Although bullion lacked the standardization (and the guarantee of quality) implicit in coinage, it had greater flexibility. In addition to imported coins, the main forms of bullion were ingots (blocks of cast metal), and cut fragments of silver, known as hack-silver (fig. 7.4). The smallest pieces of hack-silver were much smaller (and presumably less valuable) than coins, while the largest ingots were the equivalent of hundreds of coins in a single object. Quality could be tested by cutting into the surface of an object with a knife. This revealed whether or not an item was plated, and the hardness of the metal also reflected its purity, as mixing silver with lead makes it softer, while mixing it with copper makes it harder. Ingots and hack-silver are known from hoards, and from excavated sites associated with trade, as are the weights and

7.4. Piece of hack-silver, probably from a brooch. Found in Yorkshire, England. Ninth to tenth century. L. (bent) 6.1 cm. British Museum 1859,0511.6.

The Vikings in Britain and Ireland

7.5. Pieces of hack-gold from Yorkshire, England, Ninth to tenth century. Although silver was the main metal used in bullion exchange, gold was also used. Contemporary Anglo-Saxon accounts suggest that gold was around ten times the value of silver. L. 36 cm and 0.67 cm. British Museum 2010,8014.1–2.

balances used to measure them. However, the numbers of finds of all these object-types from rural areas in the UK are increasing as a result of metal detecting, indicating that bullion use was widespread, and not confined to professional traders. Detector finds have also produced increasing evidence of gold bullion, in the form of gold ingots and hack-gold (fig. 7.5). It also seems likely that copper-alloy and even lead were used in bullion exchange. The situation in the Republic of Ireland, where metal-detection is illegal, was probably similar.

Bullion was weighed using portable balances and weights. A typical balance had a pan at either end, suspended from a bar which in turn was suspended from a vertical chain or hinged bar. The main balance bar was sometimes hinged, so it could be folded into a small carrying case. The weights used fall into two main groups. One group shows the influence of the Islamic world, with standardized weights shaped like barrels, or like dice with the corners flattened off. Copies of Islamic weights were produced in Scandinavia from the late ninth century, and the idea then spread to Britain and Ireland. However, a second group of weights seems to have originated in these islands. These are lead weights with coins or fragments of metalwork set into the top, making each weight distinctive and immediately recognizable, so it was impossible to switch the weights in the course of the transaction (fig. 7.6). These more

7.6. Assorted Viking weights from England. Late ninth to tenth century. The lead weights with decorative insets are of a style developed by the Vikings in England and Ireland, while the small copper-alloy coated weights reflect the influence of the Islamic world on Viking exchange systems. British Museum.

personalized weights do not seem to have been produced to a regulated standard, but plain lead weights seem to have been issued to a common standard in Dublin in the late tenth and eleventh centuries.

Coinage and kingship

The Vikings became familiar with coins through their interactions with the Anglo-Saxons and Franks in the West, and the Islamic Caliphate and Byzantine Empire in the East. In Scandinavia, however, coins initially served as a form of bullion, alongside hack-silver and ingots, and it was only gradually that the idea took hold that coins might offer advantages over other forms of silver. This is apparent in the production of copies of Anglo-Saxon and Islamic coins, presumably in recognition of their high silver quality, which reduced reliance on quality-testing techniques. Imitative coins continued to appear in mixed bullion hoards, often with test marks. A more important development was the introduction within the Viking kingdoms of coins which had their own designs, rather than directly imitating imported coins. These first appeared in Scandinavia in the early ninth century, but they were only minted in the major trading centres of Ribe and Hedeby, with little evidence of circulation beyond the surrounding areas.

It was in England that the first major Viking coinages developed. The Anglo-Saxons who continued to live in the Scandinavian-dominated areas were already familiar with the benefits of a coin economy, and coins issued by the West Saxons served as models for the Vikings to imitate before they began to produce more distinctive designs of their own. In East Anglia there was little or no break in coin use as a result of Viking settlement, and in both northern Mercia and Northumbria the gap in minting which followed the Viking incursions was probably less than a generation.

Although familiarity with coins provided an economic argument for minting (they are an efficient system of exchange), another strong influence seems to have been exposure to Anglo-Saxon and Frankish kingship. By the time of the Viking settlements of the late ninth century, both the Franks and the Anglo-Saxons followed a model of kingship ultimately derived from the late Roman Empire, and developed under the influence of the Christian Church. One standard manifestation of royal authority within this approach to kingship was the minting of coins, which typically reflected both 'Roman' and Christian identity, with Latin inscriptions and both Christian and Roman imperial images. Diplomatic links with powerful rulers such as Alfred the Great of Wessex, as well as the influence of figures such as the archbishops of York, who managed to maintain a position of power under Viking rule, encouraged Viking kings in England to adopt a similar approach to kingship, and in turn to issue coins of their own. The first Viking ruler in England to issue coins of his own was Guthrum, who was defeated by Alfred at the Battle of Edington in 878 (see pp. 26–7), and subsequently baptized with the name of Athelstan, with Alfred as his godfather. Guthrum then established himself as king of East Anglia, and issued coins imitating those of Alfred, using his new name of Athelstan. He was followed by Guthfrith of Northumbria (died 895), who had clearly reached an accommodation with the Northumbrian Church at some point before he was buried in York Minster. This led to the establishment of a Viking coinage minted in York, with surviving examples in the names of most of the known Viking kings who had control of York, and even a few such as Cnut (*c*.900–905) and Sihtric II (early 940s), who do not otherwise appear in contemporary records (fig. 7.7). While the impetus behind the introduction of regal coinage may have been the expression of royal identity and authority, the scale of the coinage indicates that it had a real economic role in Viking England. However, unlike their Anglo-Saxon counterparts, Viking rulers in England rarely seem to have had the authority to exclude other forms of currency, and both imported coins and bullion continued to circulate after minting was introduced, except possibly in York and its immediate surrounding areas.

Not all the Christian kings of northern Europe controlled mints, and no coins were minted in Ireland, Scotland or Wales prior to the Viking settlements there. In the absence of a model of royal minting in those areas, it is unsurprising that early Viking rulers there did not issue coins of their own, despite the fact that the same dynasty had control of both Dublin and Northumbria for parts of the late ninth and tenth centuries. Kings such as Olaf Sihtricsson (died 980), who at different times had control of both York and Dublin, issued coins in the one kingdom but not

7.7. Anglo-Scandinavian silver pennies naming Viking rulers. The front and back of each coin are shown one above the other. From left to right, the coins were issued by Athelstan II/Guthrum of East Anglia (880s), Sigeferth of Northumbria (*c*.895–905), Olaf Guthfrithsson of Northumbria (939–41), Sihtric II of Northumbria (early 940s) and Eric Bloodaxe of Northumbria (died 954). Diam. (from left to right) 2.1 cm, 2 cm, 2 cm, 1.9 cm and 2.1 cm. British Museum 1838,0710.8, 1838,0710.1238, 1862,0930.1, 1848,0819. 169 and E.5081.

The Vikings in Britain and Ireland

in the other. York seems to have had a tightly controlled economy based around locally minted coins throughout the tenth century, but Dublin was able to function equally well in terms of specialized production and exchange using bullion and imported Anglo-Saxon coins. Olaf's son Sihtric Silkbeard (see pp. 117–8) eventually introduced a coinage in Dublin in the late 990s, copying the coins of Ethelred II of England (978–1016). Dublin had close economic ties with north-west England at this time, and particularly with Chester, and Sihtric's coinage probably reflects these economic links, as well as the influence of Anglo-Saxon kingship.

Ring-giving

One of the most common forms of personal ornaments to survive from the Viking Age is the arm-ring. The majority were made of silver (fig. 7.8), while gold arm-rings were both rarer and more valuable (fig. 7.9). Arm-rings came in many forms, including flat strips (often decorated with patterns of repeated punch-marks), and two or more separate bars twisted together. Others were plain, and some of these rings seem to have been produced to standardized weights, as multiples of a Viking ounce. Such rings are often referred to as 'ring-money', and functioned both as personal ornaments with a clearly defined value, and as a form of bullion currency.

The overlap between bullion value and personal ornamentation reflects the role of arm-rings in social exchange. Kings and earls would present gifts to their followers as a reward for loyal service. Suitable gifts included land, weapons, hospitality and rings. Arm-rings provided a very public display of the ties between lord and follower. They indicated both the wealth and the generosity of the giver, and generosity was one of the royal and noble characteristics most praised by contemporary poets, although they had a vested interest, as potential beneficiaries.

At the same time, the rings reflected the increased status of the recipient, and the number and size of rings provided an immediate reflection of the achievements of the wearer, as such gifts had to be earned and were not given as a matter of course. Furthermore, the rings created a lasting reminder of the relationship between giver and recipient every time they were worn. Nevertheless, as precious metal the arm-rings also had a form of monetary value; they could be disposed of or broken up for use as currency if necessary.

7.8. Silver arm-ring with punched ornament. Hiberno-Norse, ninth to tenth century, found in Scotland. Diam. 6.8 cm. British Museum OA.10303.

7.9. Gold arm-ring formed of three rods twisted together. Tenth to eleventh century. Found in Devon, England. Diam. 9.2 cm. British Museum 1979,1004.1.

The Vikings in Britain and Ireland

The Cuerdale Hoard

On 15 May 1840, workmen at Cuerdale Hall near Preston, Lancashire found a lead chest full of silver near the bank of the River Ribble. The hoard contained around 7,500 coins and around 1,000 other items (fig. 7.10), including intact ornaments, ingots and hack-silver. With a total weight of at least 40 kg, Cuerdale remains by far the largest Viking hoard from Britain and Ireland, and one of the largest from the Viking world. To put this in context, an Anglo-Saxon law code from the 920s indicates that this would have been worth around 6,000 sheep, or 1,000 oxen.

The coins in the hoard include a mixture of Anglo-Saxon coins (mostly of Alfred of Wessex, 871–99), Frankish coins from what are now France, Belgium, Germany, Italy and the Netherlands, and dirhams from the Islamic world, which stretched from Spain to Central Asia. However, the largest group was Anglo-Viking coins, mostly minted in Northumbria and East Anglia, with a few from the Midlands and some which cannot be attributed to particular kingdoms. Between them the coins date the burial of the hoard to the period AD 905–910.

The dating of this exceptional hoard raises interesting questions about why it was buried, especially as historical sources of the period say little about what was happening in north-west England at this time. In 902, the Viking leaders of Dublin were (temporarily) expelled and fled east, moving to north Wales and the Wirral, Lancashire. In 910, on the other hand, an army from Viking Northumbria suffered a major defeat at the hands of the Anglo-Saxons under Edward the Elder (899–924) at Tettenhall near Wolverhampton, so the hoard was certainly buried against a background of conflict and uncertainty in northern England and around the Irish Sea. Many of the complete and fragmentary ornaments in the hoard were produced in the Irish Sea region, while many of the coins had been minted in York. The Ribble Valley provides a natural route between the Pennines and the Irish Sea, and thus between the major Viking centres of Dublin and York. Given the importance of the Ribble Valley route, interpretations of the hoard vary between those who see it as a hoard from Ireland moving east, those who see it as a hoard from York moving west, and those who prefer to link it to a historically unrecorded power centre somewhere in the area around Preston, Lancashire. The exact circumstances behind the burial of the hoard are likely to remain a mystery.

7.10. *Overleaf* Part of the silver hoard from Cuerdale, Lancashire, buried AD 905–910. The hoard contains coins, intact ornaments, ingots and hack-silver, and originally weighed over 40 kg. British Museum 1841,0711.1–741, 1873,1101.1; 1954,0202.1–2; 1838,0710.1436, 1442, 1168, 1203. Donated by HM Queen Victoria in 1841, in her capacity as the Duke of Lancaster.

Kings and things: Viking society

Viking society was strictly hierarchical. Powerful rulers controlled the wealth – land, produce and the proceeds of raiding and trading – and were supported by an aristocracy, who, when necessary, led military forces to defend them and to further their territorial ambitions. These forces were manned from the class of freemen – farmers and merchants who held land on a small scale, and who were allowed to bear weapons, and attend and speak at assemblies where administrative and legal matters were settled. At the very bottom of the hierarchy were slaves, individuals who were the property of others, with no legal rights.

Textual, archaeological, and place-name evidence usually tells us only about the relatively wealthy members of Viking-Age society. Even grave-goods such as tools, often seen as evidence of the activities of 'ordinary' people, were only deposited in the graves of the same wealthy men and women (fig. 5.9).

8.1. King from a group of chess pieces found on the island of Lewis, probably made in Norway in the late twelfth century. Compare fig. 2.4. The sword reflects the role of the king as warleader in Viking society, but the fact that he is seated on his throne rather than actually wielding his sword suggests the king's other roles as the fount of law and government. Walrus ivory. H. 9.9 cm. British Museum 1831,1101.79.

Everyone except slaves enjoyed legal rights, and English legal documents suggest that, from the tenth century, certain areas of Scandinavian settlement had a legal identity distinct from elsewhere in Anglo-Saxon England. The phrase *on De(o)ne lage* 'under the Danes' law' occurs twice in a legal document from the reign of Ethelred II (978–1016), and an earlier lawcode of Edgar (959–75) refers to rights and laws *mid Denum* 'among the Danes' as 'they best decide upon' ('Danes' referring broadly to those whose identity was in some way Scandinavian). The fact that 'Danish' legal provisions are outlined in Anglo-Saxon documents is evidence that they fall under the legislative authority of England, a fact underlined by another part of the Edgar code which states that 'Englishmen and Danes and Britons' everywhere in the kingdom are subject to the measure that 'poor man and rich may possess what they rightly acquire.'

Kings

The term 'king' meant different things in the course of the Viking Age, not least because it was used in different ways by the Vikings and some of their neighbours. Across much of western Europe kings were rulers of specific geographical areas, or of specific peoples, even if the boundaries of their kingdoms might change. England, Ireland and Wales were all divided into multiple kingdoms at the beginning of the Viking Age, while Scotland as we know it today was divided into the Scottish kingdom of Dalriada in the west, and the rival kingdom of the Picts in the east.

A similar pattern can to some extent be seen in the Viking homelands. At the beginning of the Viking Age, Scandinavia was divided into many small kingdoms and peoples, each with a king of its own (pp. 11–13). These kings often acted as war-leaders, but also had a role in imposing the rule of law, and in some cases, if not all, had a spiritual role, leading their people in sacrifices and other forms of deity-worship. However, kingship could also be a matter of personal status, and it was possible for men of royal blood to claim the title of king even if they did not rule a specific people or territory, as long as they could persuade enough people to recognize their title.

8.2. Stone cross from Middleton, North Yorkshire, England. Tenth century. On the shaft is an image of what appears to be a warrior wearing a pointed helmet, surrounded by a full set of 'Viking' weapons – sword, spearhead, axe and shield. In addition, he may be holding a long knife. The arrangement of these weapons recalls some Viking furnished graves (see fig. 5.8). It is important to understand that weapons were symbols of rank and authority as well as military ability. The individual commemorated on this cross was clearly an important landowner. H. 175.5 cm. York Archaeological Trust.

This probably applied to many of the leaders of the Viking forces who attacked Britain and Ireland. The Viking army defeated at Ashdown, Sussex in 871 was led by at least two kings and five earls, and the 'Great Army' which came to Cambridge in 874 was led by three kings, Guthrum, Oscytel and Anund. None of these is identified as ruler of a particular kingdom. Similarly, when Eric Bloodaxe was killed in 954, five other kings were supposedly killed with him, although the evidence for this is late and unreliable.

In the course of the ninth and tenth centuries the Vikings established new territories for themselves in Britain and Ireland. Kingdoms were established in the Western Isles of Scotland, the Isle of Man, and around the Hiberno-Norse towns, particularly Dublin and Waterford. A major dynasty, the *Uí Ímair* ('Descendants of Ivarr') became rulers of Dublin and, intermittently, the former Anglo-Saxon kingdom of Northumbria, with a number of kings ruling at different times in both

8.3. Illustration of Cnut and his wife Emma, widow of the English king, Ethelred II. From the *Liber Vitae* of the New Minster, Winchester, England. Cnut and Emma are seen as patrons of the Church, and Cnut is portrayed as an Anglo-Saxon king, despite his Danish origins. Parchment, 1031. L. 26 cm; W. 15 cm. British Library, Stowe 944, f.6.

Dublin and York. The Vikings also took control of East Anglia and parts of Mercia, and by the end of the ninth century Wessex was the only Anglo-Saxon kingdom to have survived the Viking onslaught. It was the rulers of Wessex who pushed back the boundaries of the Scandinavian-controlled areas of England until, by the mid tenth century, there was something approaching a single unified English kingdom (pp. 29 and 51). It was this unified kingdom whose throne was seized, following a period of intense raiding, first in 1013 by the Danish king, Svein Forkbeard, who died shortly afterwards, and then in 1016 by his son, Cnut the Great, undoubtedly the most powerful king to have emerged from Viking-Age Scandinavia.

Cnut ruled England from 1016 to his death in 1035, and added to this Denmark (from 1019), and parts of Norway (1028–34). England was the centre of his empire, and there his reign brought with it a period of stability and prosperity, largely free from the intense raiding that characterized the preceding reign of Ethelred II. Despite the rapid despatch of several members of the English aristocracy, who had enjoyed a high level of power under Ethelred, Cnut's interest in maintaining a certain level of continuity was signalled with his marriage to Emma, Ethelred's widow. The new king took pains to be seen as a Christian ruler and a generous patron of the church (fig. 8.3) – his mode of kingship is scarcely comparable with that enjoyed by the kings of the early Viking Age, whose control of much smaller territories was far less secure.

Sihtric Silkbeard, king of Dublin

Perhaps because of his unusual epithet, Sihtric Silkbeard (Old Norse *silkiskeggi*) is easily the best-known of the Viking kings of Dublin. His father, Olaf Sihtricsson, who had the Irish nickname *Cuarán* (literally 'sandal'), seems to have been the first Christian king of Dublin, and his mother, Gormlaith, was the daughter of the local Irish king of Leinster. Sihtric became king of Dublin in 989, just as the career of the upstart Bórama ('Boru') was taking off, and he successfully negotiated the resulting political minefield which culminated in the Battle of Clontarf, fought just outside Dublin in 1014 (see p. 37). He seems to have avoided participating in the battle himself and came to terms with the new political realities which followed Brian's death, surviving as King of Dublin until 1036. He spent the last six years of his life in exile, possibly in north Wales.

Sihtric's long, if occasionally interrupted, reign of some 47 years saw major developments in Dublin. The latest and most substantial of the defensive earthen banks uncovered at Wood Quay (p. 95) was constructed *c*.1000 and reflects the wealth and power of the growing town, as well as a possible English influence – town defences being relatively common there by this time. More secure evidence for Anglo-Saxon connections is provided by the coinage which Sihtric introduced to Dublin *c*.997 (fig. 8.4) which was modelled on contemporary English pennies. Despite occasional attacks, Dublin prospered as a commercial centre during his long reign, although it should also be remembered that the city continued to engage in military campaigns with various Irish allies. In 1028, Sihtric returned from a pilgrimage to Rome, and soon afterwards established a cathedral at Dublin, arranging for the city's first bishop to be consecrated at Canterbury – a tradition which was to continue for well over a century. In this and other ways, Sihtric was a truly 'Hiberno-Norse' ruler, at home in Irish, Scandinavian, and indeed Anglo-Saxon environments.

Earls

Not all Viking rulers took the title of king. In later medieval and modern times, those holding the position of earl were subordinate to kings, and this pattern seems also to have been adopted in the later Viking Age. At an earlier date, it was apparently possible for earls to function as independent rulers. An 'Earl Sihtric' issued coins in his own name in Cambridgeshire around AD 900, several towns in the Midlands of England were ruled by earls, and one of the most powerful and enduring Viking territories in the British Isles was the earldom of Orkney, established from Norway in the late ninth century. *Orkneyinga saga*, or 'saga of the Orkney Islanders' (also known as *Jarla saga*, 'the

8.4. Silver penny of Sihtric Silkbeard, minted in Dublin, *c*.1000. The design copies contemporary pennies of Ethelred II of England (978–1016), issued in the late 990s. Diam. 1.8 cm. British Museum 1986,1201.1.

The Vikings in Britain and Ireland

saga of the Earls'), paints a vivid picture of the lives of the Orkney earls, albeit from the perspective of its early thirteenth-century Icelandic author. The earls engaged in raiding elsewhere in Britain and Ireland, and in bitter struggles for power at home, with brother pitted against brother and cousin against cousin, and treachery a feature of everyday life. The women who married into this dynasty were no less scheming, and wielded formidable, if indirect, power. The saga-author paints an unflattering picture of one Ragnhild, daughter of Eric Bloodaxe and despatcher of multiple husbands. Ragnhild engineers the death of her husband, Earl Arnfin, then marries his brother Earl Havard. She persuades one nephew, Einar, to kill Havard, then another to kill Einar, and finally marries Earl Ljot, brother of Arnfin and Havard.

8.5. Bronze key. Uncertain findspot. Ninth to eleventh centuries. Keys are a common element in female burials, signifying the role of the lady of the house in controlling household expenditure, and her access to valuable stored supplies. L. 15 cm. British Museum 1967,0609.1.

Viking women

Runic evidence from across mainland Scandinavia suggests that Viking-Age women from powerful families could exercise considerable authority in less violent ways than Ragnhild – they both commissioned and were commemorated by expensive memorial stones. The runic inscriptions also reveal that, in the absence of surviving male relatives, they could inherit fortunes. The runestones from the Isle of Man on the other hand, which reflect a mixed Norse-Celtic environment, name women only as dedicatees, not as commissioners (fig. 4.3). Evidence of their wielding power and accruing wealth is therefore lacking, even though it is clear that the women commemorated in death were valued. Elsewhere in Britain and Ireland we have no such inscriptions, but a number of place-names in England contain Scandinavian female names, recording women who held land or were in some other way associated with particular places. These have to be treated with care as a Scandinavian personal name does not necessarily indicate a person of Scandinavian origin or descent. Rather, it may reflect a fashion for such names – the name Gunnhild, for example, was very popular in parts of England well into the thirteenth century. Nevertheless, the variety of women's names of

The Vikings in Britain and Ireland

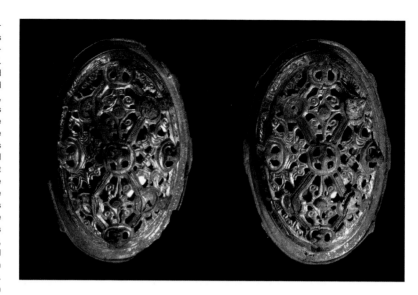

Scandinavian linguistic origin in medieval England suggests a substantial female population arriving from Scandinavia. The Gunnvor whose name is preserved in the place-name Gunnerton, Northumberland, the Mothir in Motherby, Derbyshire, and the Sigrith in Sizergh, Cumberland, if not themselves Scandinavian must have been so-called from a name-stock which was current in England, and this currency is best explained as the result of a substantial female population bearing these names, arriving in England from Scandinavia at some point during the Viking Age.

What other evidence might support the idea of Scandinavian female immigration? There is relatively little to be found in historical texts, although the *Anglo-Saxon Chronicle* tells us of a Viking leader called Hæsten, who sailed into the Thames in 892 and established a base at Benfleet, Essex. When this was stormed by the English, they captured not only its treasures but women and children too, including Hæsten's wife and two sons, who were taken to King Alfred in London. Archaeologically, the most striking find in England is the grave of a mature Viking woman, discovered in 2001 at Adwick-le-Street in Yorkshire. She had been buried, probably in the late ninth century, in clothes fastened by the oval brooches characteristic of Viking-Age women in Scandinavia, and with a knife, a key, and a bronze bowl. Analysis of her tooth enamel suggests that she had been born and raised in Norway (or just possibly north-east Scotland), and was therefore an incomer to the area.

In other areas of Britain and Ireland, the archaeological evidence is richer. There are notable female burials at Ballyholme, in County Down, Ireland, Barra in the Western Isles of Scotland (pp. 80–81) and Westness, on the Orkney island of Rousay. As at Adwick, each woman was buried with oval brooches and a range of other objects, including copper-alloy bowls, but both the Westness woman, who was buried alongside a newborn baby, and the Barra woman were accompanied by artefacts associated with weaving – an important status-related skill in this period. Scotland is particularly rich in female graves: at Pierowall on Westray, six of seventeen Viking-Age furnished graves contained oval brooches, and are therefore probably those of Viking women.

Legal practices

How were the legal practices of these distinctively 'Danish' areas implemented? Scandinavian areas of England were divided into *wapentakes* (from the Old Norse *vápnatak* meaning 'taking of weapons') – administrative and legal divisions which served much the same range of functions as their English equivalents, the hundreds. Each *wapentake* would have held a regular assembly at a designated meeting place, and smaller divisions within the *wapentake* would also have had regular local meetings. It was at such meetings that legal procedures were implemented. The names of the meeting-places often record this important legal and administrative function: there are numerous place-names which contain a word indicating a gathering, often compounded with a second element indicating (in origin) a distinctive landscape feature. We find in northern and eastern England many places called *þing-haugr* 'assembly-mound' (the *þ* denotes a 'th' sound), *mot-haugr* 'meeting-mound', *spell-haugr* 'speech-mound', and *þing-vǫllr* or *-vellir* 'assembly-field(s)'. This last name-type is found across Scandinavia and also numbers among its constituent sites Þingvellir, where the Icelandic

8.8. *Overleaf* Tingwall Holm, Shetland. The name is derived from Old Norse *þing-vǫllr*, meaning 'assembly-field', and *holmr*, meaning 'island'. Tingwall Holm, the island in the centre of the picture, was the meeting place of the Shetland law assembly for many centuries.

The Vikings in Britain and Ireland

8.7. Tynwald Hill on the Isle of Man. Manx culture has been subjected to many influences, including the Vikings. The Manx parliament is still called the Tynwald, and meets ceremonially on the Hill on 'Tynwald Day' (every 5 July), although regular meetings are now held indoors.

national assembly gathered until 1798. Examples are to be found in Scotland and the Isle of Man as well as England: Tingwall (Shetland, Orkney – fig. 8.8), Tinwald (Dumfriesshire), Dingwall (Ross-shire), Thingwall (Wirral, Lancashire) and Tynwald (Isle of Man – fig. 8.7). In Ireland, *Thengmotha*, immediately east of the walled city of Dublin, survived as a place-name until at least the thirteenth century.

Slaves

Legal rights and processes were inaccessible to the lowest stratum of society – slaves. The moveable wealth sought by Viking raiders included not only gold and silver, but also people. Among the many entries in the Irish annals that record the plunder and bloodshed wrought by the

Vikings – with increasing accounts of Irish victory – are some which detail the taking of prisoners. For example, in 821, twenty-six years after the first recorded Viking raid on Ireland in 795, 'a great number of women' were snatched from the Howth peninsula, north of Dublin, and taken into captivity. In 836, the Vikings 'carried off many prisoners, and killed many, and led away very many captive' from the kingdom of Brega (now part of County Meath). In 895, the number of prisoners is given: 710 were taken into captivity following raiding on Armagh. The Irish were not the only victims: in 871, Ivarr and Olaf, the kings of Dublin, returned from the British kingdom of Strathclyde with 'a great prey of Angles, Britons and Picts'.

These captives would have been valuable commodities, many of them destined to be traded. People so far down the social scale generally leave little trace in the archaeological record, but excavations in Dublin uncovered what may be a Viking-Age 'slave' collar (fig. 8.9), and a crude carving on a broken piece of slate found on the island of Inchmarnock, off the west coast of Scotland, may show a slave led by one of three men wearing mail shirts (fig. 8.10). Famously, the practice of slave-sacrifice is detailed in the account of a Viking chieftain's funeral in Russia by the tenth-century Arab writer Ibn Fadlan: he describes the multiple rape

8.9. Possible slave collar from Dublin. Tenth to twelfth centuries. Similar artefacts have been found at some high-status Irish sites. Some have suggested that they were used to bind particularly important captives or hostages. As the poorest members of Scandinavian – and indeed Irish and Anglo-Saxon – society, slaves have left few, if any traces in the archaeological record. Diam. 15 cm. National Museum of Ireland.

The Vikings in Britain and Ireland

and murder of a drugged slave-girl during the ceremony. A number of Viking-Age graves contain two individuals, one of whom appears to have been killed in order to accompany the deceased on the journey beyond death – these graves likely provide grisly evidence of slave-sacrifice. They include an example at Ballateare on the Isle of Man, where a young man was buried with his weapons in a pit beneath a mound. In the upper levels of the mound was the skeleton of a young woman without grave-goods, who seems to have been killed by a sword blow to the back of her head, delivered while she was kneeling down.

The textual and archaeological record for people from the British Isles taken into slavery by Vikings has been supplemented in recent years by genetic evidence. Studies on the modern population of Iceland, which was settled from around the 870s onwards, suggests that around 80% of the early female settlers and around 20% of the early male settlers were from the 'Celtic' areas of the British Isles, rather than from Norway, the homeland of most of the wealthy individuals detailed in the (later) historical accounts. A fair few of these are likely to have been slaves.

8.10. 'Hostage stone' from the island of Inchmarnock on the west coast of Scotland, c.800. This piece of graffiti appears to show a chained prisoner being led away by men in mail shirts. It may represent the Viking practice of taking prisoners either as slaves or as hostages for ransom. L. 12cm; W. 18 cm. National Museums Scotland.

The Viking legacy

The Viking Age did not come to a sudden or abrupt end. Although major events like the Battle of Stamford Bridge in 1066 and the death of Magnus Barelegs in Ireland in 1103 (see p. 11) formed significant milestones in the political history of these islands, the mixed populations in many areas of Viking settlement remained in place, and contacts with Scandinavia remained strong throughout the Middle Ages. This was especially true in Scotland, where the kings of Norway and the archbishops of Trondheim maintained a direct interest in the north and west of the country, and trading links were close. Throughout these islands, the former Viking settlements only gradually assimilated into the emerging countries which now form the United Kingdom and the Republic of Ireland. Even after centuries of assimilation, the Viking legacy is strong in many places. This legacy is clearly written on the signposts of much of northern England, parts of Scotland, and to a lesser extent of Wales and Ireland. It is to be heard in the Scandinavian loanwords which pepper the everyday English of these islands' present-day inhabitants, and is to be seen in various material remains, increasingly the focus of the heritage industries.

Genetics

There is a further, less visible manifestation of Scandinavian heritage which in recent years has offered a new way to assess the impact of the Vikings: the traces they have left in our DNA (deoxyribonucleic acid), the genetic code which is passed down through the generations from parents to children. The vast majority of our DNA is a complex mixture of that of our parents, which is a complex mixture of that of their parents and so on, such that it becomes impossible to know which section comes

THORESWAY 2½ TEALBY 2
CAISTOR 5¼ WILLINGHAM 4½

STAINTON LE VALE 1¼ WALESBY 1
BINBROOK 4¼ MKT RASEN 3½

9.1. On this Lincolnshire signpost, Scandinavian place-names like Walesby (Val's village) and Thoresway (possibly 'shrine dedicated to Thor') nestle with ancient English names such as Willingham ('homestead of the Wifelingas'). See also fig. 4.7.

from which distant ancestor. However, there are two segments of our DNA that have a very simple pattern of inheritance. The first of these is the sex-determining Y-chromosome – the reason men are male – which is passed down from father to son. The Y-chromosome of a man living in the twenty-first century will look very much like that of his father, and like the Y-chromosome of that man's father, and so on, right back through time. Also with a simple pattern of inheritance, this time just through the female line, is mitochondrial DNA, which is passed down from a mother to her children of both sexes, although only daughters will in turn pass it to their children. The mitochondrial DNA of a person living in the twenty-first century will have been passed down through the generations from a distant maternal ancestor. It is therefore possible to get a glimpse of one line of a woman's ancestry – only one among many – by examining her mitochondrial DNA, or, if male, a glimpse of two lines – again, two of many – by examining both his mitochondrial DNA and his Y-chromosome.

Not all Y-chromosomes and mitochondrial DNA are the same. Little changes, known as mutations, occur in the DNA sequence as it is being copied to be passed down into sperm or egg. These mutations result in there being different types of mitochondrial DNA and Y-chromosomes. The sites where DNA sequences are known to differ between individuals are known as markers.

A number of these markers can be used to divide Y-chromosomes and mitochondrial DNA into broad types, known as 'haplogroups'. These haplogroups have particular geographical distributions – they are characteristic of certain populations in certain parts of the world. This non-random distribution means that analysis of these elements of the genetic codes of individuals living in the twenty-first century has the potential to tell us something about the origins and movements of past populations – including the movement of Vikings out of Scandinavia to Britain and Ireland and elsewhere.

Genetic studies of the last decade have compared Y-chromosome types commonly found today in Norway with those of men from various parts of Britain whose grandfathers also came from the same place. (This 'two-generations criterion' attempts to get around the problem of very recent population movements.) Statistical analysis has revealed relatively high proportions of Scandinavian ancestry in the present-day (male) populations of the Northern and Western Isles, parts of the north and west of Scotland, the Isle of Man, and parts of the north-west of England. This has been interpreted as an indication of a significant Norwegian Viking contribution to the DNA of that male population. Similar research in Ireland, on the other hand, has so far failed to detect any such contribution.

Comparable studies on other parts of the Viking world have also cast light on Viking activities in the British Isles. Analysis of the modern population of Iceland, for example, has suggested that a high proportion of Iceland's women have a maternal ancestor who originated not in Norway but in the British Isles – a significantly higher proportion than for the men, whose DNA suggests a predominantly Norwegian ancestor

The Vikings in Britain and Ireland

population. Here, science seems to confirm what historical and literary texts record: the Irish annals give stark accounts of women snatched by raiding Vikings, and later Icelandic historical and literary writings afford a place to individuals from Britain and Ireland in the settlement of Iceland (see p. 127). DNA has thus become a useful tool for exploring the genetic legacy of the past in modern populations, at least in terms of wider trends. However, it is of more limited value in establishing the identity of modern individuals, as it is currently only possible to trace one branch (for a female) or two (for a male) on a genetic family tree that has hundreds of millions of branches extending back over the thousand years since the late Viking Age. And aside from this, the ability to trace genetic trends across populations in different regions depends entirely on the willingness of individuals to allow their DNA to be tested.

A new portrayal

Until comparatively recently Vikings stood outside the national narratives that dominated the study of the history in these islands, and consequently 'Viking' heritage was both underestimated and under-emphasized. At best, Vikings were presented as villains who destroyed monasteries or opposed patriotic kings such as Alfred the Great. The rehabilitation of the Vikings has been a long and slow process, inspired both by the nineteenth-century romantic tradition and by ongoing archaeological excavations which have pointed to major Viking achievements. Today, the Vikings are generally portrayed in a positive light that our great-grandparents would have found distinctly odd.

Many tourist centres emphasize the role of the Vikings as town founders. The Jorvik Centre, for example, was set up to celebrate the Viking heritage of York revealed by excavations at Coppergate, and it remains one of the most popular heritage attractions in the UK (fig. 9.2). At Dublin, the Dublinia Centre has also embraced the city's Viking heritage, while Waterford is currently developing a 'Viking Triangle' of heritage institutions which echoes the layout of the original Viking settlement. Reconstructions of urban 'Viking' houses can also be found

at a number of Heritage Parks, and in those areas where stone sculpture survives, principally northern England and the Isle of Man, the sculptures have become tourist attractions in their own right. In general, however, tangible Viking remains take the form of portable artefacts, and it is perhaps in museum galleries that visitors come closest to the physical remains of the Viking past.

These same remains have inspired reconstructions and re-enactment by enthusiasts, and continue to fascinate the wider public. Viking remains have also inspired the construction of a series of replica ships and boats, primarily at the Viking Ship Museum, Roskilde, Denmark (fig. 1.8). These and other activities celebrate the role of the Vikings in bringing together disparate parts of northern Europe and the North Atlantic, as well as the vibrant diversity of Viking culture – Hiberno-Norse, Scotto-Norse, or Anglo-Scandinavian. Viking heritage is as diverse as the groups whose raiding, trading, and settlement created the Viking world.

As this book has highlighted, we are now acutely aware of the role of Vikings as settlers, farmers and traders, but still, scholars are only just beginning to understand the complexity of their engagement with

The Vikings in Britain and Ireland

indigenous communities and kingdoms across Britain and Ireland. Future research will continue to refine our understanding of their contribution to the rich heritage of these islands.

The Viking image has never been more popular, although it remains divided between views of the Vikings informed by recent scholarship, and the stereotypical image of the bearded warrior with horned helmet. This creates an interesting tension for heritage sites and museums trying to promote an accurate sense of the Vikings, but facing commercial pressure to meet popular expectations, horned helmets and all. The Jorvik Viking Centre largely presents the more peaceful aspects of Viking settlement and crafts to the public, but for years ran a line of merchandise with a warrior image and the caption 'Eric Bloodaxe rules OK?'. The image is traditionally wild and bearded, but does wear a reasonably authentic helmet (without horns), as does the 'Viking duck' for children marketed by the British Museum (fig. 9.3).

The popularity of Vikings is further reflected by the widespread use of the 'Viking' name and imagery to sell a variety of goods and services. In some cases this is directly linked to the tourist industry, not just in museums and heritage sites, but in places with any sort of Viking association. Largs in Ayrshire, Scotland, site of the last Norwegian invasion in 1263, has a Viking fish and chip shop, while York has a Viking handicraft shop. Other businesses have no direct association with heritage, but nonetheless use the Viking name or image to promote a sense of power, speed, strength or dynamism. These vary from the Viking ship logo of Rover cars to Viking businesses selling everything from hand-dryers to office stationery. Viking heritage is also explored through a number of annual Viking-themed festivals in areas with Viking associations, although like Viking-themed merchandising, these often reflect Viking stereotypes as well as, or instead of attempting to explore the genuine Viking heritage.

9.3. Viking-themed bath duck. This is one of a range of historically-themed ducks produced for children by the British Museum, and is identifiable as a Viking from the characteristic helmet, beard, axe and shield.

Finally the more personal appeal of the Vikings can be seen in the thousands of people involved in Viking re-enactment. The popularity of historical re-enactment has grown steadily since the 1960s, and the Viking Age is one of the most popular periods, with two large national societies in the UK, as well as many other groups and societies across Britain, Ireland, Scandinavia, and the rest of the world. Re-enactment is often used to support the heritage industry, but re-enactment events often occur in places with any sort of Viking associations (fig. 9.4). Like Viking merchandising, the authenticity of how Vikings are portrayed in re-enactment varies enormously, and people become involved for many different reasons, of which an interest in history is only one. The sense of community, the exhilaration of (safety-monitored) battle, and the opportunity to travel and escape from daily routine are perhaps not so different from those which helped to inspire ship-loads of young men 1200 years ago to go a-viking.

9.4. The festival of Up-Helly-Aa has been celebrated in Lerwick in Shetland since the late nineteenth century. The festival takes place in January, and involves a torchlit procession in romanticised Viking costumes, culminating in the burning of a Viking ship.

The Vikings in Britain and Ireland

Timeline

5th century	Beginning of Anglo-Saxon settlement of England from Denmark, northern Germany and neighbouring areas
7th century	Similarities in metalwork from Sutton Hoo and other Anglo-Saxon objects indicate continued contact with Scandinavia
c. 789	First recorded Viking attack on England, near Portland in Dorset
793	Viking attack on monastery at Lindisfarne, Northumbria. Usually taken to mark beginning of Viking Age
794–5	Attacks on monasteries in Northumbria, Ireland and Scotland
837	Ireland 'devastated' by the raiding of churches, monasteries and shrines
841	*Longphuirt* established at Dublin and Linn Duachaill (Annagassan)
850	Vikings over-winter for the first time in England
865	Arrival of 'Great (Heathen) Army' in East Anglia, England
870	Dubliners under Olaf and Ivarr besiege Dumbarton Rock, Scotland (successfully)
871	'Great slaughter' of Vikings at Ashdown, Sussex by West Saxons under Ethelred I and Alfred. Alfred succeeds his brother as king
876	Settlement of Northumbria by the 'Great Army'
878	Defeat of Vikings under Guthrum by Alfred at Edington. Guthrum adopts Christianity and settles in East Anglia
902	Viking rulers expelled from Dublin
914	Great fleet lands at Waterford, re-establishing Viking activity in Ireland
917	Viking dynasty reinstated in Dublin
927	Athelstan conquers Viking Northumbria to create unified kingdom of England
937	Athelstan defeats alliance of Scots, Vikings and Strathclyde British at *Brunanburh*
939	Death of Athelstan and restoration of independent Viking Northumbria
954	Death of Eric Bloodaxe, last king of Northumbria
970s	Viking rulers of the Isle of Man active around the Irish Sea
989	Mael Sechnaill, king of Meath, imposes an annual tax on the men of Dublin
991	Viking victory at Maldon in Essex marks the beginning of a new phase of large-scale raiding in England
c.997	Introduction of locally minted coinage in Dublin
1013	Svein Forkbeard of Denmark conquers England
1014	Battle of Clontarf, between the kings of Munster and Leinster, with Viking allies on both sides
1016	Cnut, son of Svein Forkbeard, becomes king of England
c.1030	Bishopric established at Dubllin
c.1035	Thorfinn the Mighty, earl of Orkney, extends authority over parts of northern and western Scotland
1042	Death of Harthacnut, son of Cnut. End of Danish rule in England
c.1050	Bishopric established in Orkney
1058	Magnus, son of Harald Hardruler of Norway raids around the Irish Sea
1066	Unsuccessful invasion of England by Harald Hardruler of Norway, killed at Stamford Bridge, together with the earls of Orkney. Successful invasion of England under William of Normandy
1103	Magnus Barelegs, king of Norway, killed while raiding in Ulster
1170	Anglo-Norman forces allied with Diarmait Mac Murchada, king of Leinster, take Waterford and Dublin

Further reading

Ballin Smith, B., Taylor, S. and Williams, G. (eds), *West over Sea: Studies in Sea-borne Expansion and Settlement before 1300*, Leiden and Boston: Brill 2007

Batey, C., Jesch, J. and Morris, C.D. (eds), *The Viking Age in Caithness, Orkney and the North Atlantic*, Edinburgh: Edinburgh University Press 1993

Blackburn, M.A.S., *Viking Coinage and Currency in the British Isles*, British Numismatic Society Special Publications 7, London: Spink/British Numismatic Society 2011

Brink, S. and Price, N. (eds), *The Viking World*, Abingdon: Routledge 2008

Clarke, H.B, Ni Mhaonaigh, M. and Ó Floinn, R., *Ireland and Scandinavia in the Early Viking Age*, Dublin: Four Courts 1998

Crawford, B.E., *Scandinavian Scotland*, Leicester: Leicester University Press 1987

Downham, C., *Viking Kings of Britain and Ireland: The Dynasty of Ívarr to A.D. 1014*, Edinburgh: Dunedin 2007

Edwards, B.J.N., *Vikings in North West England*, Lancaster: University of Lancaster 1998

Faulkes, A. (trans.), Snorri Sturluson, *Edda*, London: Dent 1987, reprinted regularly since

Findell, M., *Runes*, London: British Museum Press 2014

Graham-Campbell, J. et al (eds), *Cultural Atlas of the Viking World*, Oxford: Andromeda 1994

Graham-Campbell, J. and Batey, C.E., *Vikings in Scotland: An Archaeological Survey*, Edinburgh: Edinburgh University Press 1998

Graham-Campbell, J. and Philpott, R., *The Huxley Viking Hoard: Scandinavian Settlement in the North West*, Liverpool: National Museums Liverpool 2009

Graham-Campbell, J., Hall, R., Jesch, J., and Parsons, D.N. (eds), *Vikings and the Danelaw*, Oxford: Oxbow 2001

Graham-Campbell, J.A., Sindbæk, S.M. and Williams, G. (eds), *Silver Economies, Monetisation and Society in Scandinavia, 800–1100*, Århus: Aarhus University Press 2011

Graham-Campbell, J.A., *Viking Art*, London: Thames & Hudson 2013

Griffiths, D., *Vikings of the Irish Sea: Conflict and Assimilation AD 790–1050*, Stroud: History Press 2010

Hadley, D.M., *The Vikings in England: Settlement, Society and Culture*, Manchester: Manchester University Press 2006

Hadley, D.M., and Richards, J.D. (eds), *Cultures in Contact: Scandinavian Settlement in England in the Ninth and Tenth Centuries*, Turnhout: Brepols 2000

Hadley, D.M. and Ten Harkel, L. (eds), *Everyday Life in Viking-Age Towns: Social Approaches to Towns in England and Ireland, c.800–1100*, Oxford: Oxbow 2013

Harrison, S.H., and Ó Floinn, R., *Viking Graves and Grave-Goods in Ireland*, Dublin: National Museum of Ireland, *forthcoming* 2014

Holman, K., *The Northern Conquest: Vikings in Britain and Ireland*, Oxford: Signal 2007

Hall, R., *Viking Age York*, London: Batsford 1994

Hall, R., *Exploring the World of the Vikings*, London: Thames & Hudson 2007

Hines, J., Lane, A., and Redknap, M. (eds), *Land, Sea and Home: Settlement in the Viking Period*, London: Society for Medieval Archaeology 2004

Jesch, J., *Ships and Men in the Late Viking Age: The Vocabulary of Runic Inscriptions and Skaldic Verse*, Woodbridge: Boydell 2001

Jesch, J., *Women in the Viking Age*, Woodbridge: Boydell 2005

Jesch, J., *Viking Poetry of Love and War*, London: British Museum Press 2013

Johnson, R., *Viking Age Dublin*, Dublin: Town House 2004

Kershaw, J., *Viking Identities: Scandinavian Jewellery in England*, Oxford: Oxford University Press 2013

Larsen, A.C. (ed.), *Vikings in Ireland*, Roskilde: The Viking Ship Museum 2001

Orchard, A., (trans.), *The Elder Edda: A Book of Viking Lore*, London: Penguin 2011

Page, R.I., *Chronicles of the Vikings*, London: British Museum Press, reissued 2014

Price, N., *The Viking Way: Religion and War in Late Iron Age Scandinavia*, Uppsala: Dept of Archaeology and Ancient History 2002

Redknap, M., *Vikings in Wales: An Archaeological Quest*, Cardiff: National Museums and Galleries of Wales 2000

Richards, J.D., *Viking Age England*, Stroud: Tempus 2000

Ritchie, A., *Viking Scotland*, London: Batsford 1993

Roesdahl, E., *The Vikings*, London: Penguin 1987

Sawyer, P. (ed.), *The Oxford Illustrated History of the Vikings*, Oxford: Oxford University Press 1997

Sheehan, J., and Ó Corráin, D. (eds), *The Viking Age: Ireland and the West*, Dublin: Four Courts 2010

Townend, M., *Language and History in Viking Age England: Linguistic Relations Between Speakers of Old Norse and Old English*, Turnhout: Brepols 2002

Valante, M., *The Vikings in Ireland: Settlement, Trade and Urbanisation*, Dublin: Four Courts, 2008

Williams, G., *The Viking Ship*, London: British Museum Press 2014

Williams, G., Pentz, P. and Wemhoff, M. (eds), *Vikings: Life and Legend*, London: British Museum Press 2014

Wilson, D.M., *The Vikings in the Isle of Man*, Århus: Aarhus University Press 2008

Picture credits

Index

The Vikings in Britain and Ireland